How to use this book

Children develop skills at different times and this book is designed to support them as they grow and learn. The pen control and writing activities will allow children to practise holding a pen and the sticker activities will encourage fine motor skills.

Holding a pen

Encourage your child to hold a pen in between the thumb and the index finger, a little above the tip, with a gap in between. Left-handers should hold the pen slightly further up from the tip, as shown in the picture.

The pen should be resting on the middle finger to support it. It should be easy for your child to move the pen up and down by moving those three fingers only.

Right hand or left hand

You probably know by now which hand your child favours. If not, this book will help. You will probably notice better pen control with one, although some people are happy to use both.

Hands should be relaxed.

Don't press down too hard.

Perfect posture

It is best for your child to sit at a flat table or desk, feet on the floor with back straight. For right-handers, the book should be at a slight angle, on the right side of your child's body. For left-handers, the book should be positioned at more of an angle on the left side of the body, with the top left corner about two inches higher than the right.

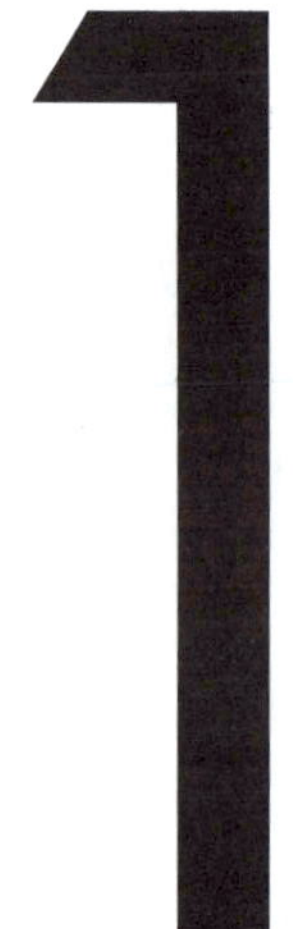

look at the number

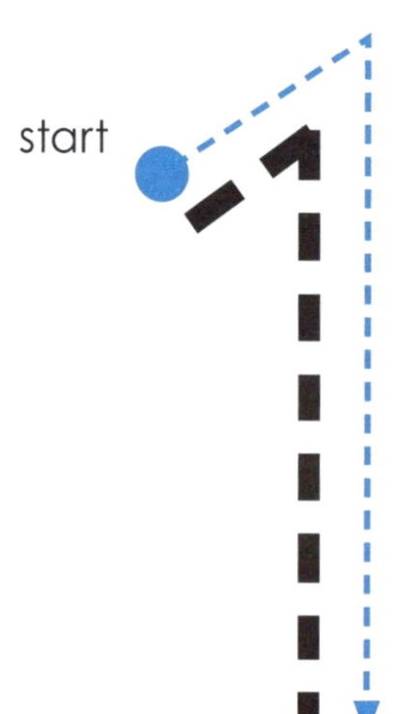

trace the number

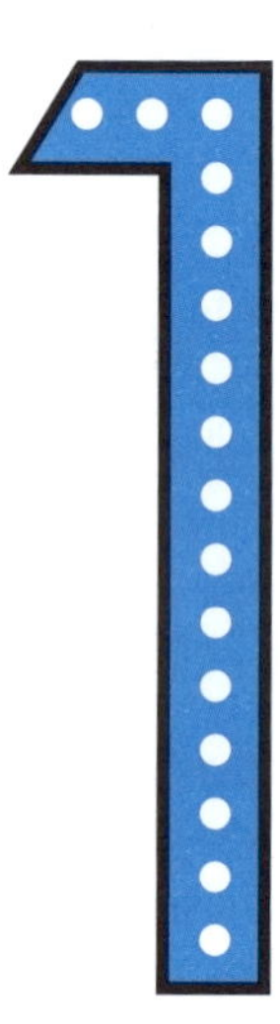

write inside

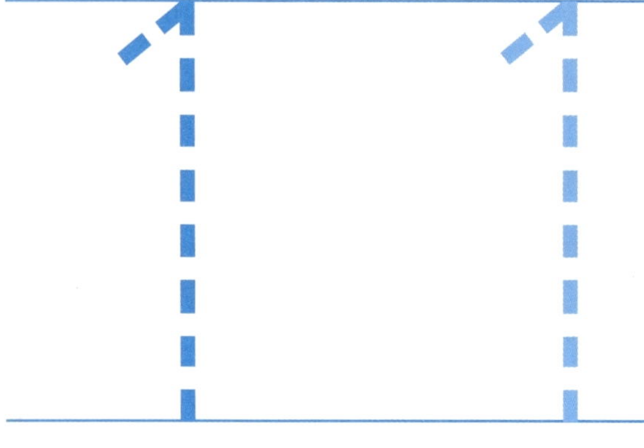

Keep your hand steady to draw a straight line.

number practice

2

2
motorbikes

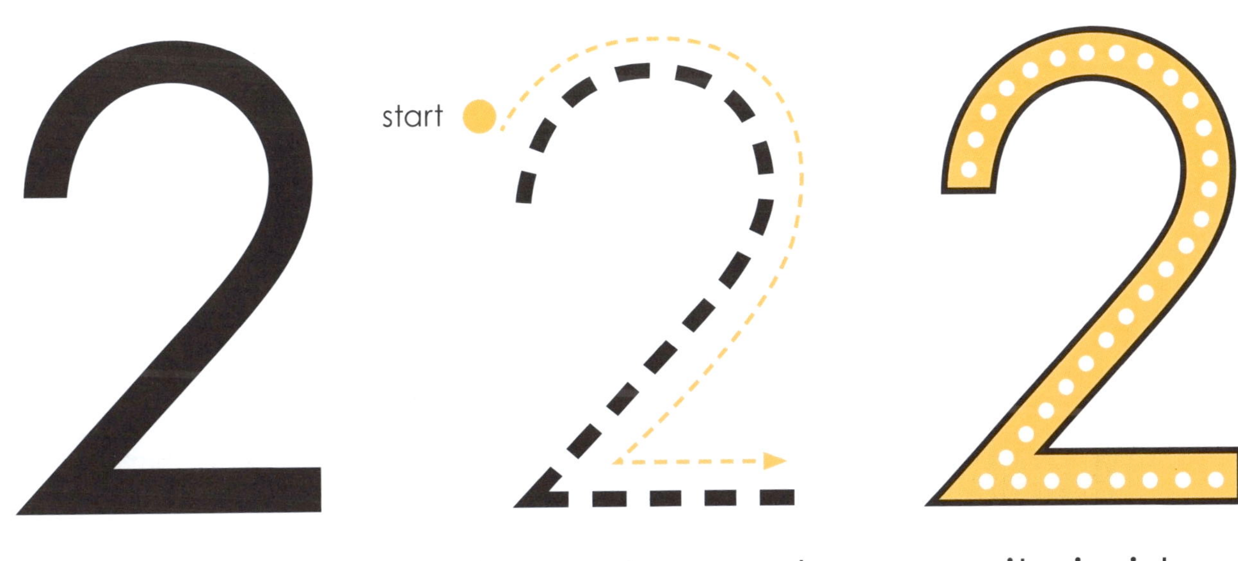

look at the number trace the number write inside

number practice

3

3
cows

look at the number   trace the number

write inside

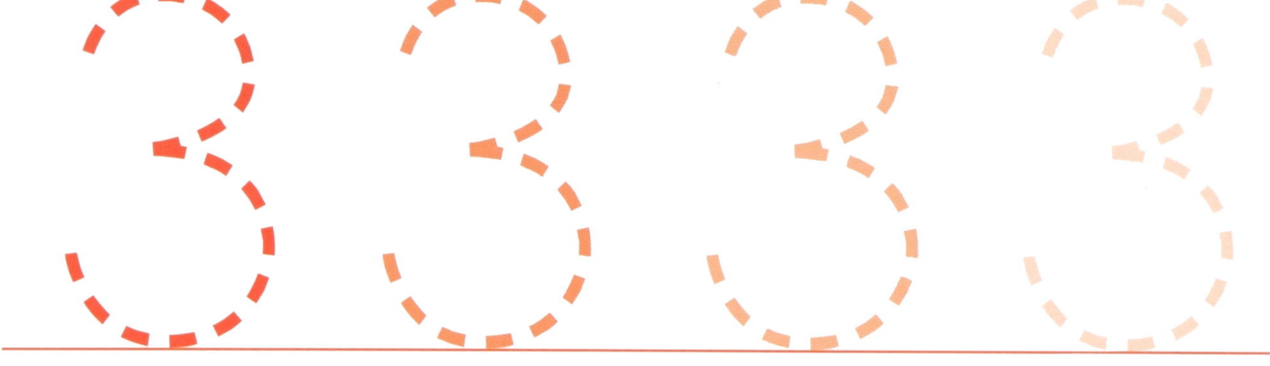

number practice

4

4
trucks

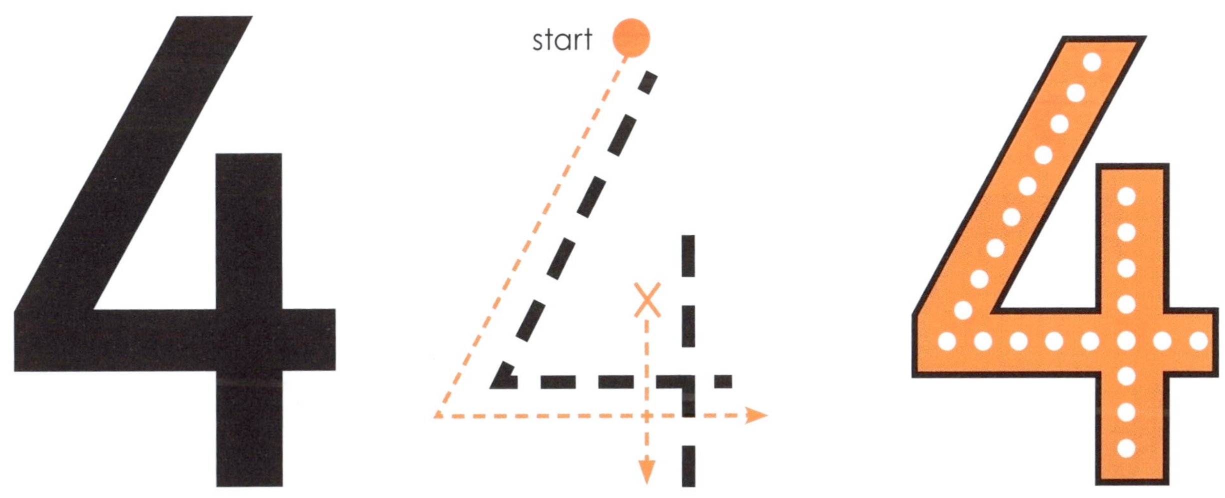

look at the number | trace the number | write inside

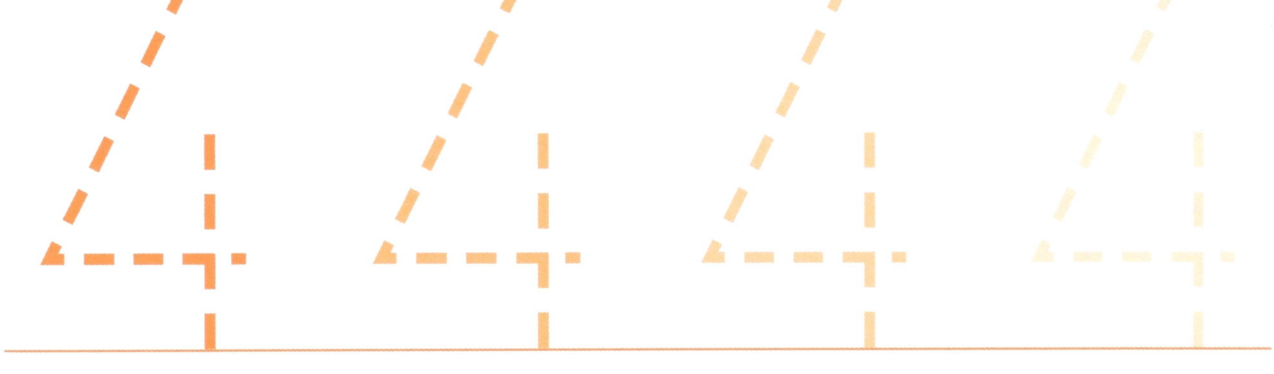

You need to draw two separate lines to form the number four.

number practice

look at the number trace the number write inside

number practice

6
horses

look at the number

trace the number

write inside

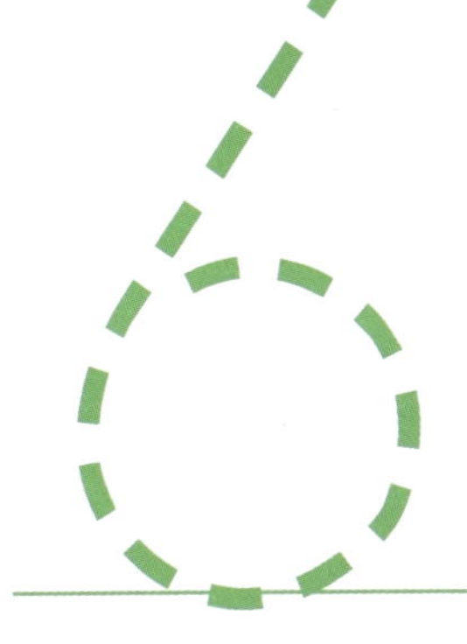

number practice

7
puppies

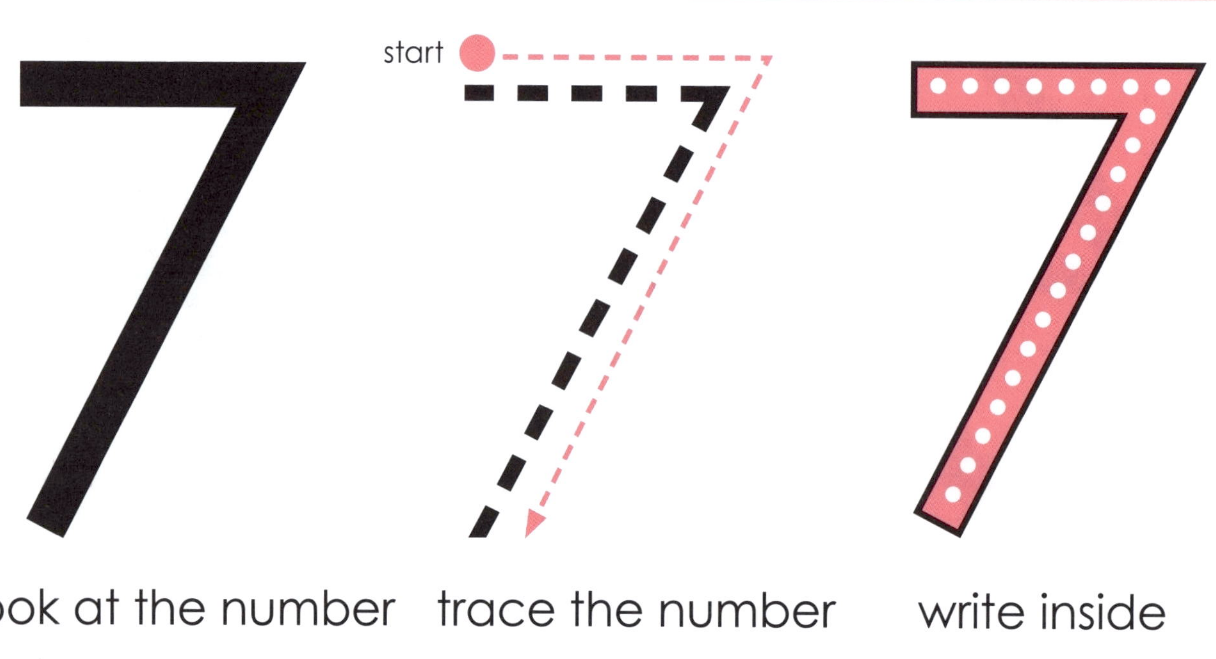

look at the number trace the number write inside

number practice

8

vegetables

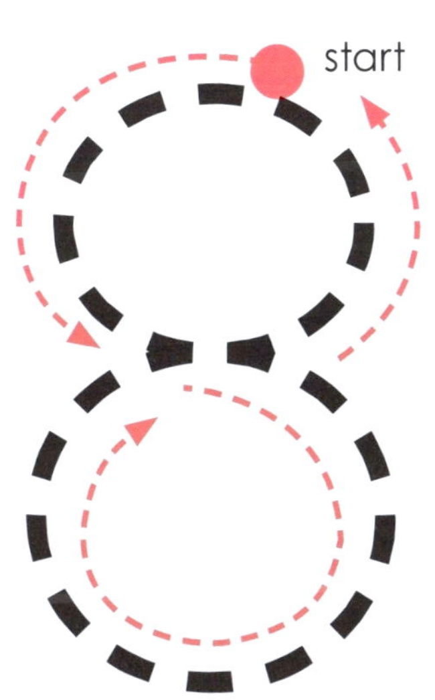

look at the number trace the number write inside

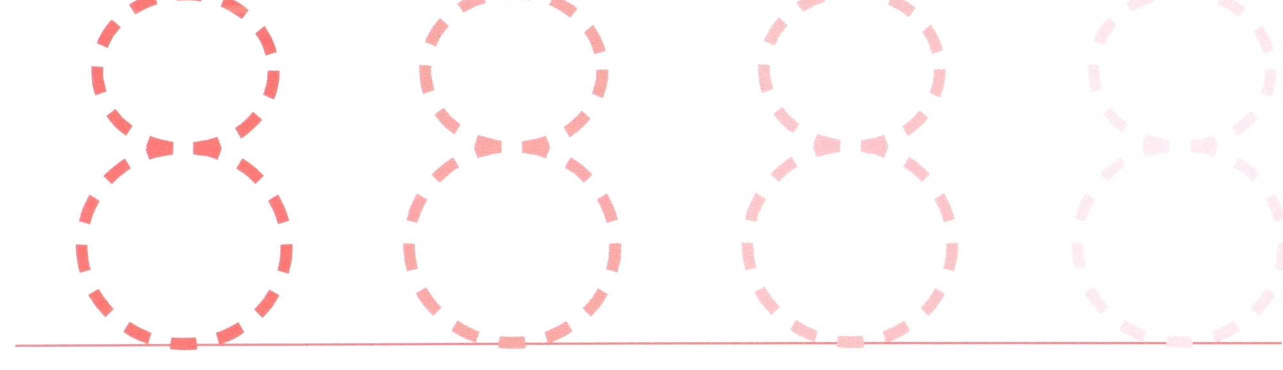

number practice

look at the number

trace the number

write inside

number practice

10

10
fruits

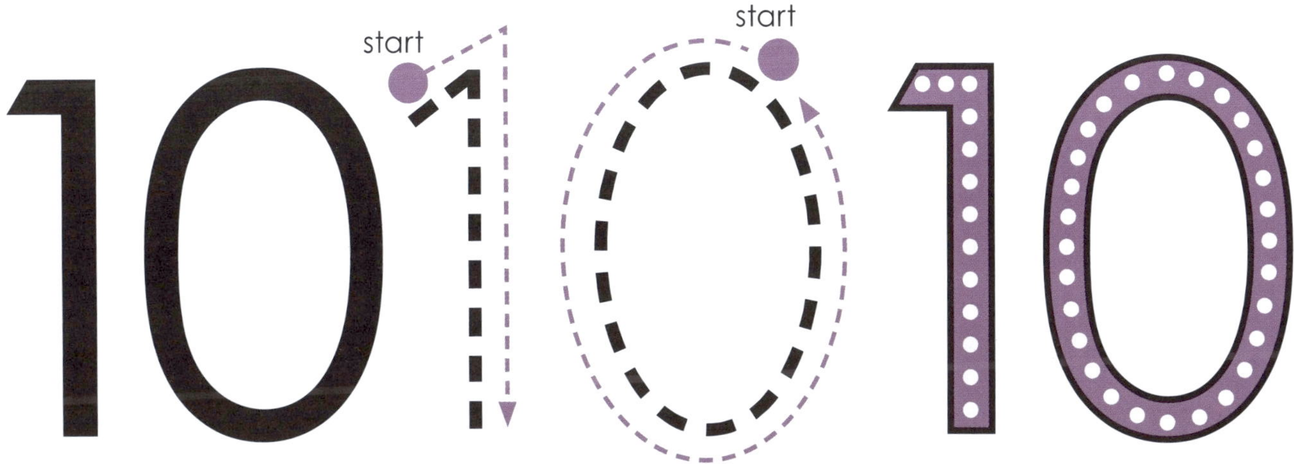

look at the number trace the number write inside

number practice

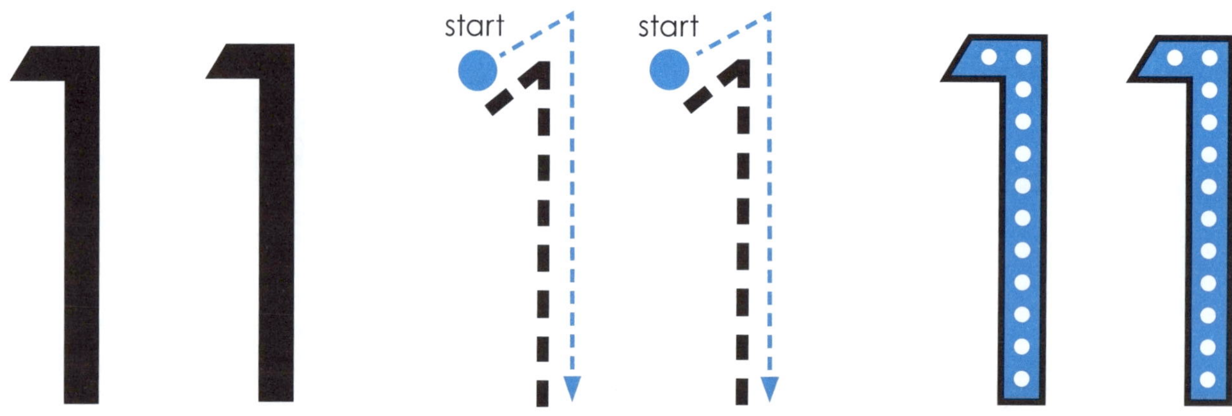

look at the number trace the number write inside

number practice

12
fish

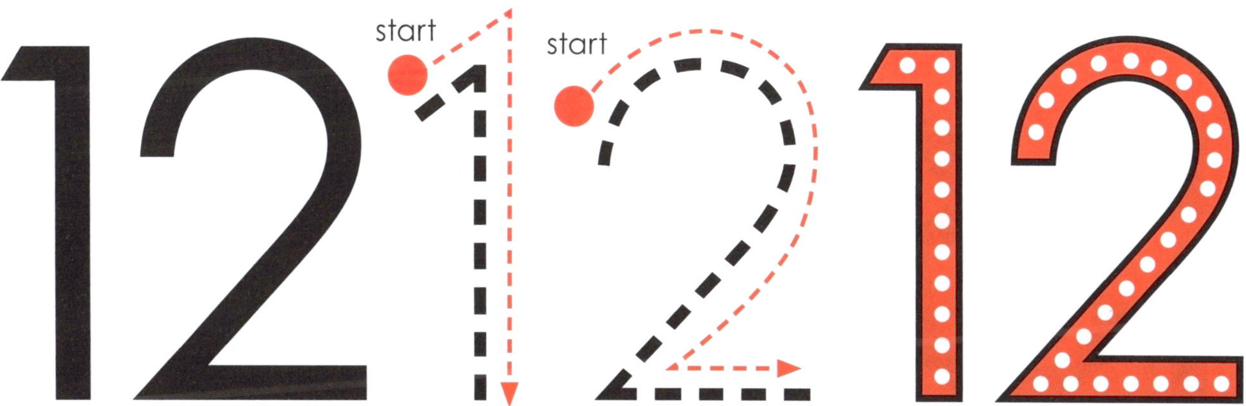

look at the number trace the number write inside

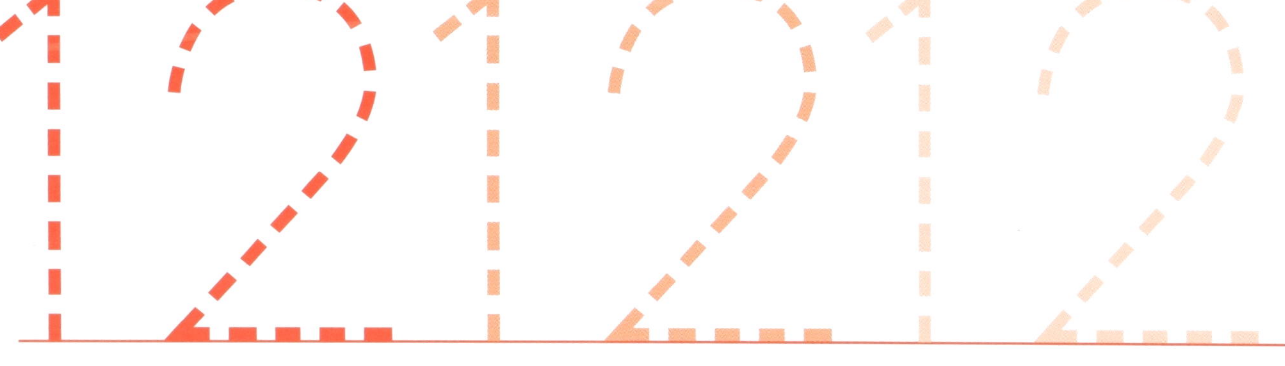

number practice

13
chicks

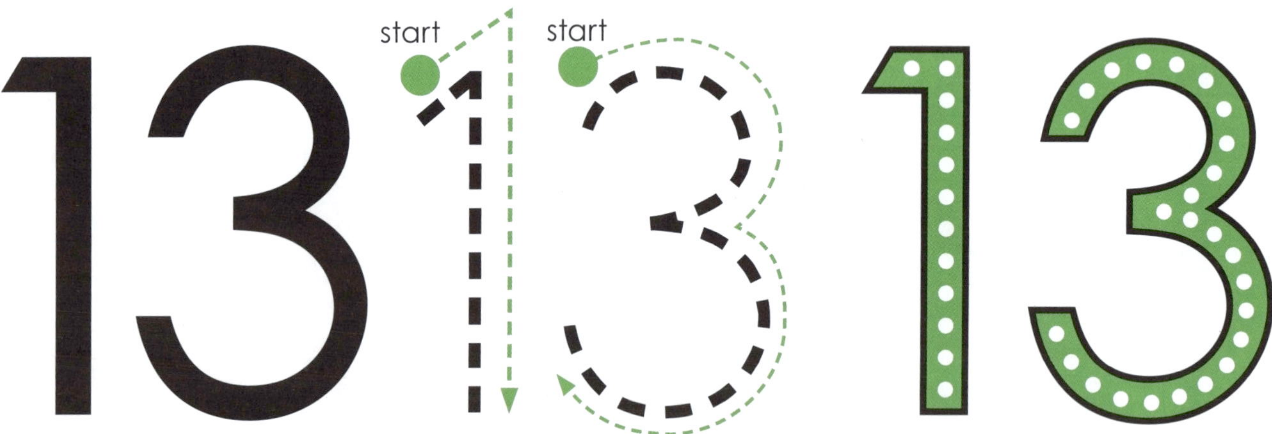

look at the number trace the number write inside

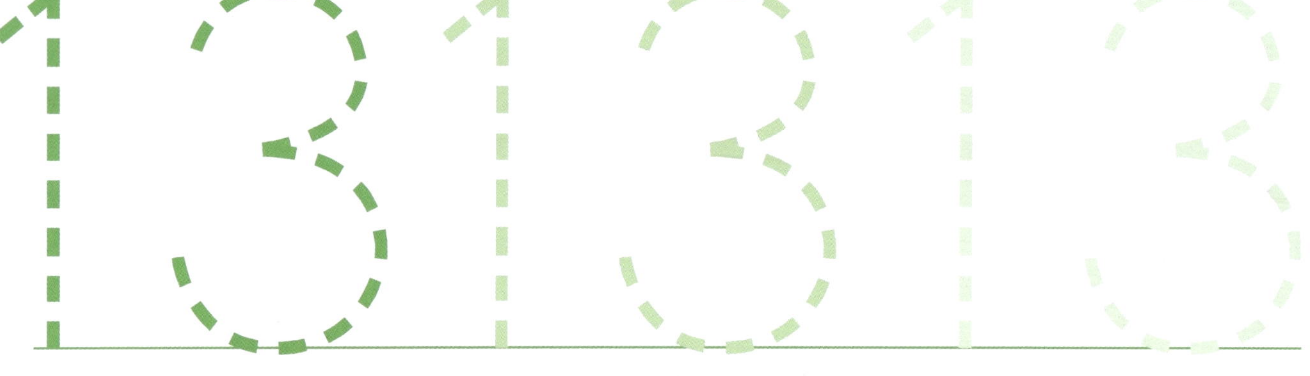

number practice

14

14
hats

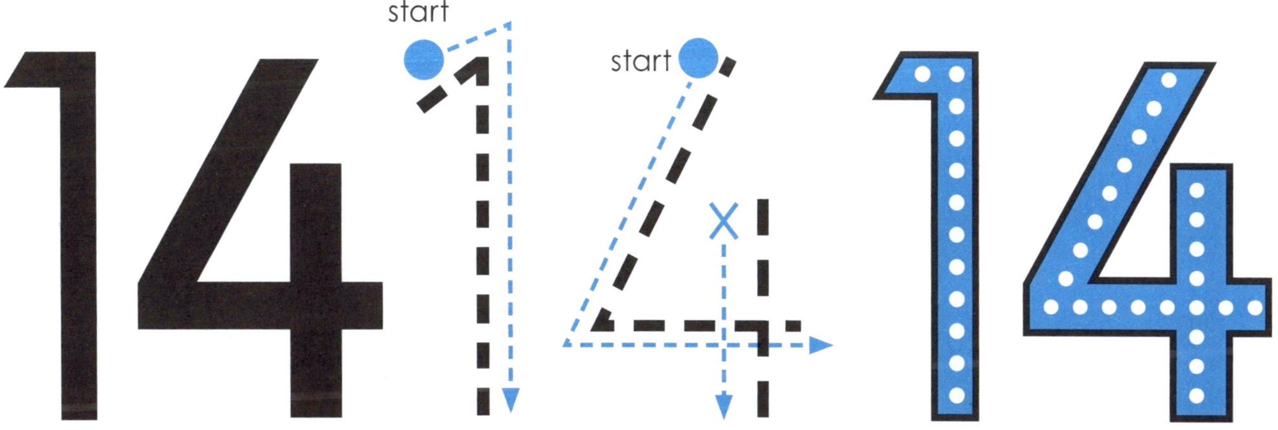

look at the number trace the number write inside

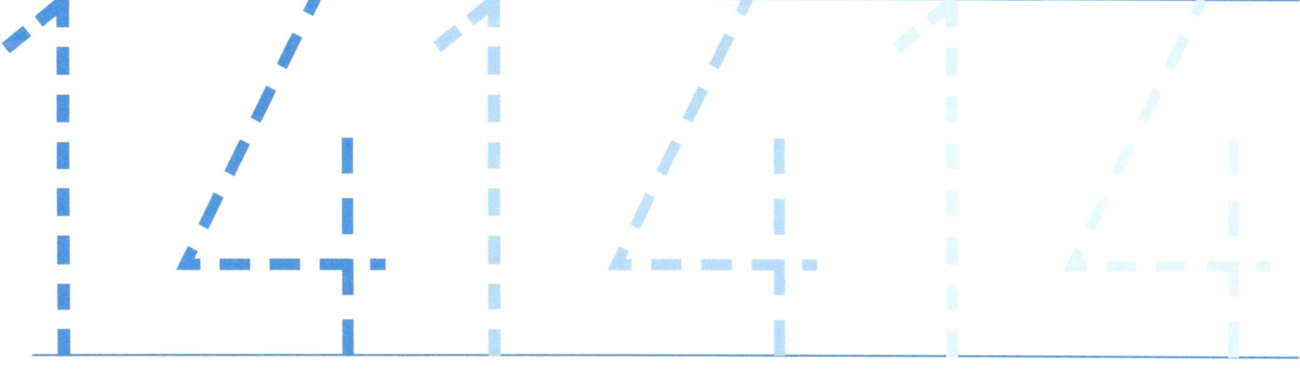

number practice

15

15
leaves

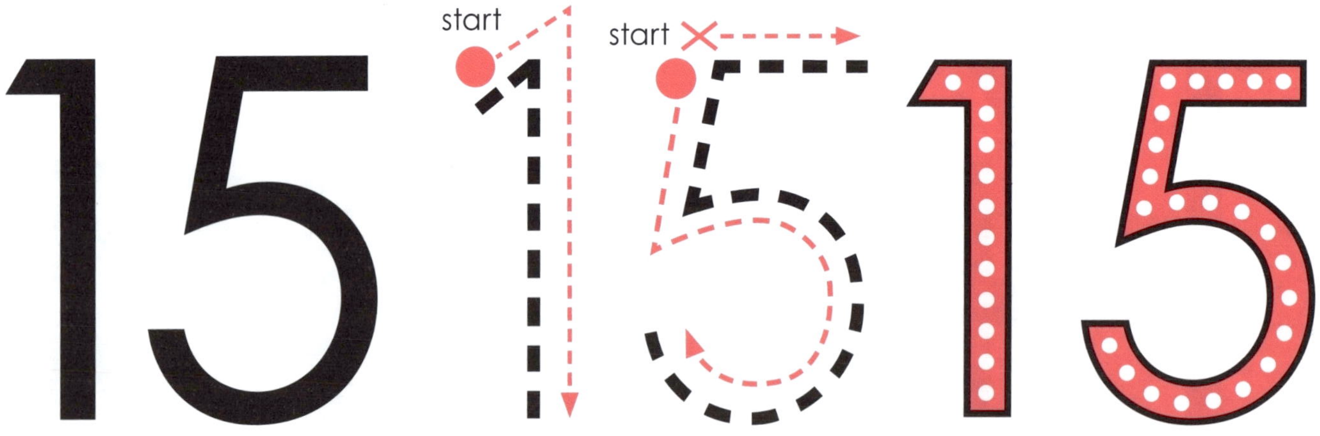

look at the number trace the number write inside

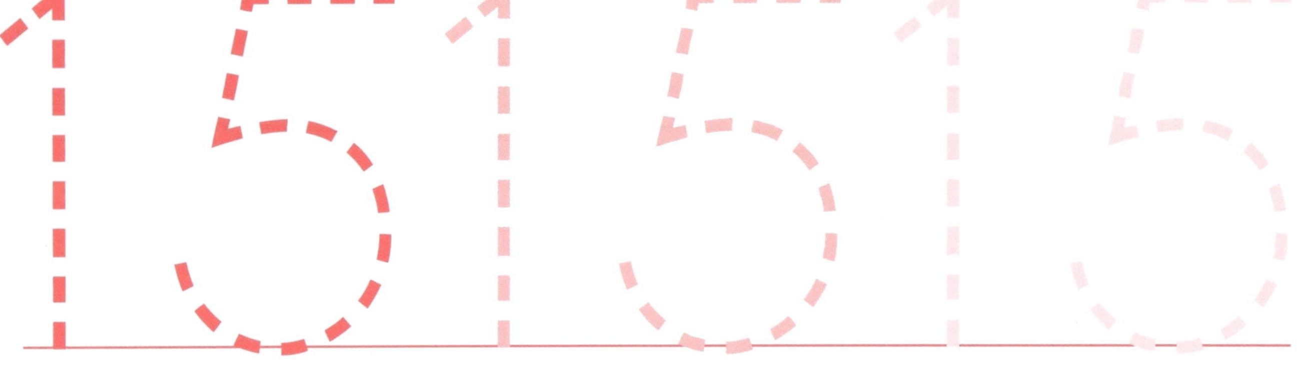

number practice

16
balloons

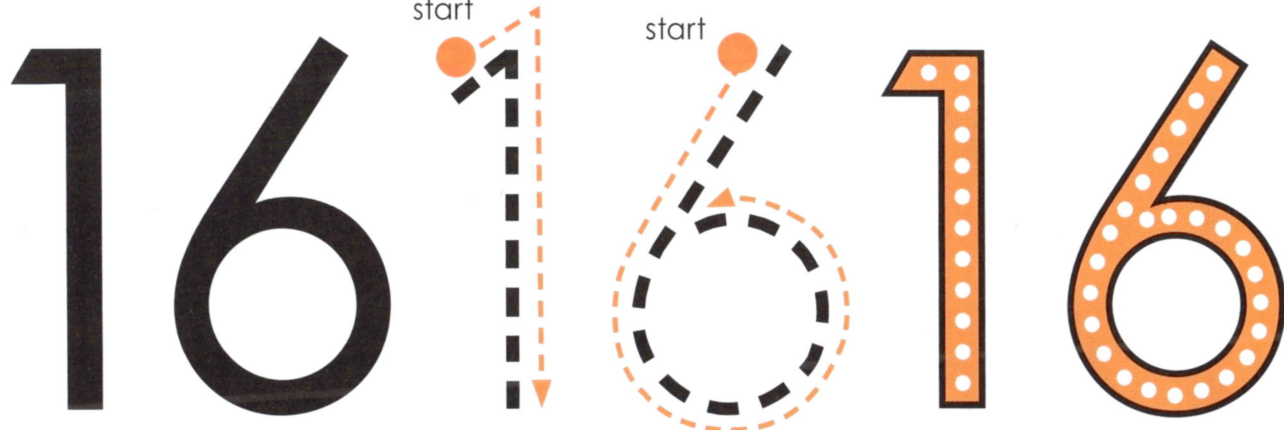

look at the number trace the number write inside

number practice

17

17
sweets

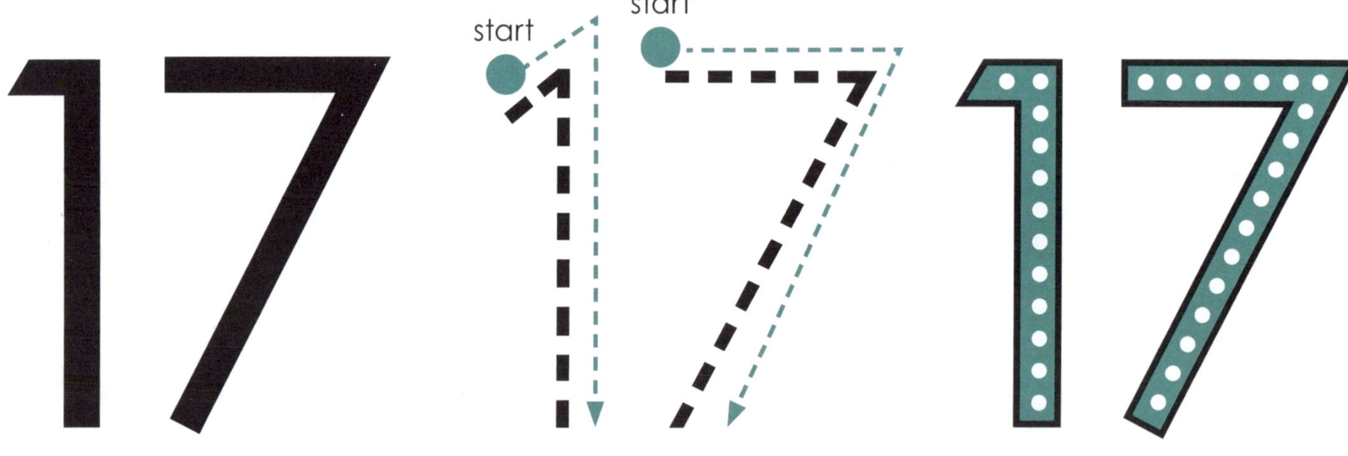

look at the number trace the number write inside

number practice

18

18
flowers

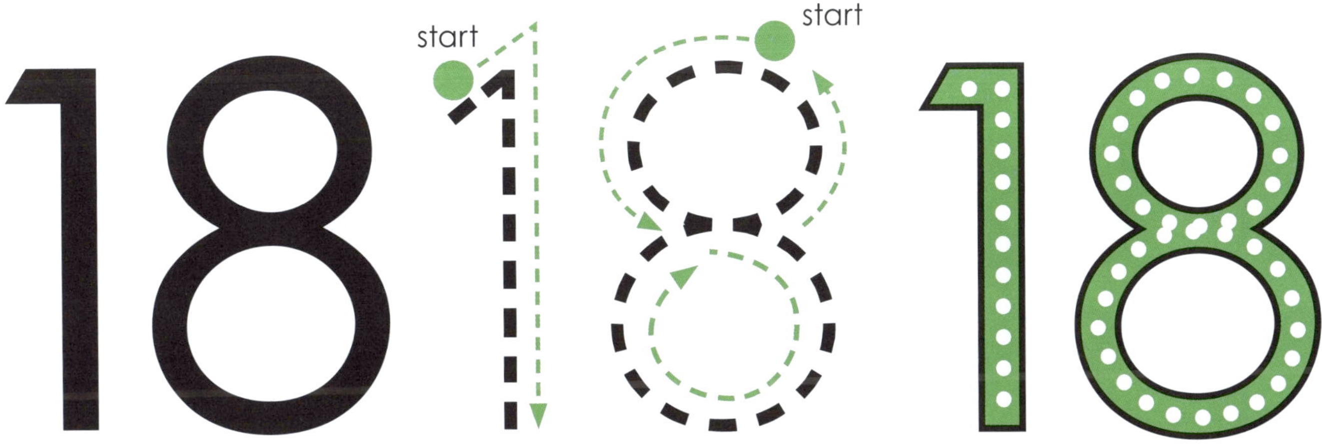

look at the number trace the number write inside

number practice

19

19 balls

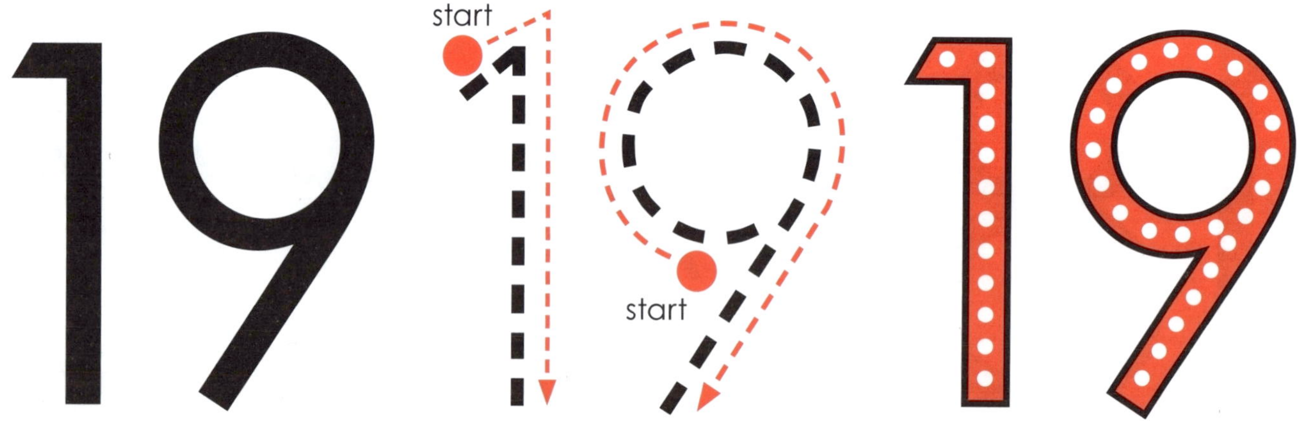

look at the number trace the number write inside

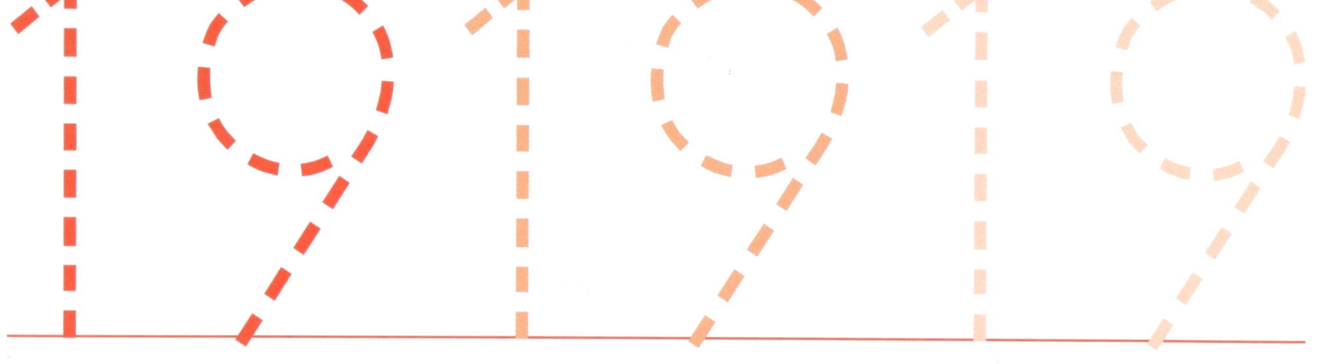

number practice

20

20
bath ducks

look at the number trace the number write inside

number practice

Clock work

Trace over the numbers already on the clock, then fill in the missing ones!

Count them up!

Count the number of items in each group, and then write the number in the box below.

colourful bowling pins

candles on a cake

peas in a pod

spots on a mug

Linking numbers

Trace the numbers, and then draw a line between each vehicle to connect the numbers in the correct order.

Market day

Count each group of fruit, and then write the correct number on the sign above it.

Number spotting

Circle all the numbers in the grid from 15 to 20.

11	16	2	8	10	15
16	19	3	12	18	1
7	13	17	13	9	14
10	15	2	3	8	11
19	5	20	4	1	3
2	7	17	19	6	12

Writing numbers

Trace over the numbers and words.

teddy bear

1 one

trucks

2 two

dolls

3 three

toy soldiers

4 four

dinosaurs

5 five

Quack! Quack!

Colour in the cute scene below.
How many ducklings are at the pond today?

Matching numbers

Count each group of objects, trace over the numbers and match the two together!

Counting clothes

Colour in all the different types of clothing.
How many woolly hats can you count?

Find and count

Can you find and count the items below?
Tick the boxes as you find them.

1 cosy bed	☐	5 blue chairs	☐
2 mirrors	☐	6 clocks	☐
3 strawberries	☐	7 apples	☐
4 lamps	☐	8 pink socks	☐

Catching butterflies

How many butterflies can you count?
Then colour in all the pictures.

Picture sequences

Colour in the last picture in each row to finish the pattern.

Number bonds

Using your pen, trace the numbers below.
Follow the direction of the arrows.

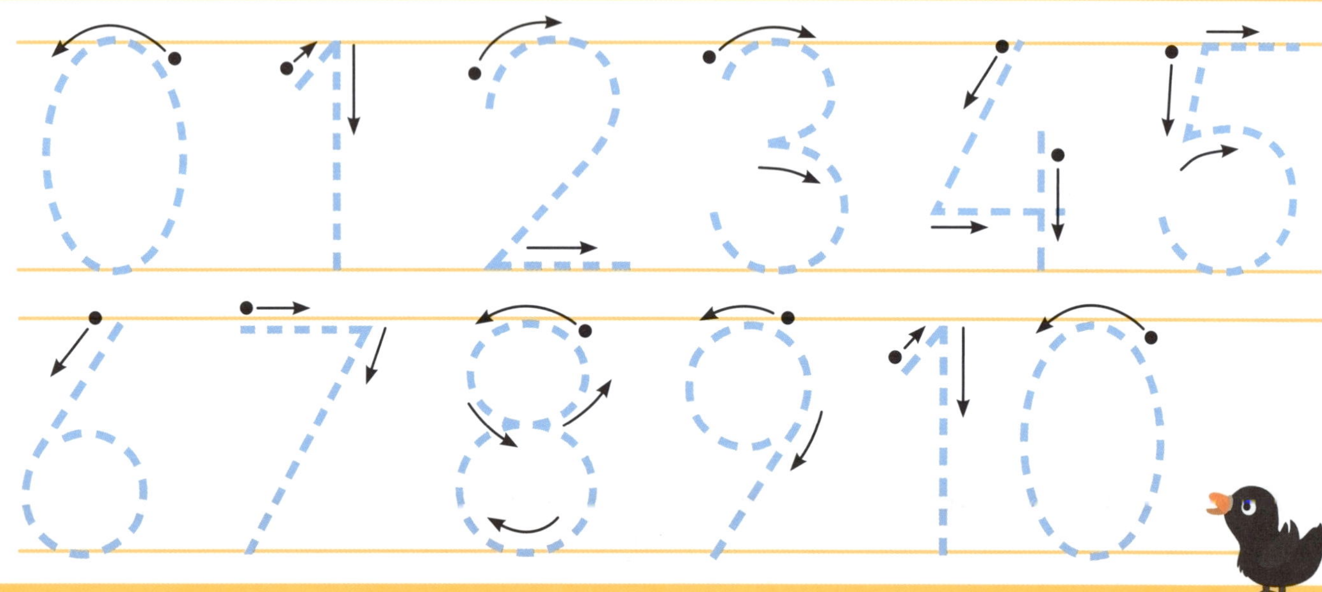

The number bonds to 10 are all the numbers that when added together make 10. Now try to trace them.

0 + 10 = 10

Trace this number bond.

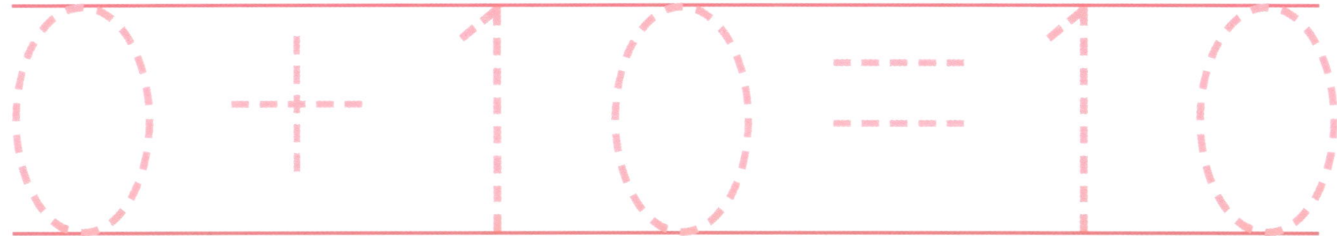

Count the children and complete the sum below.

0 children + 10 children = 10 children

This leopard has no spots!

Can you draw 10 spots with your pen?

Practise this number bond.

☐ + ☐ = 10

1 + 9 = 10

Trace this number bond.

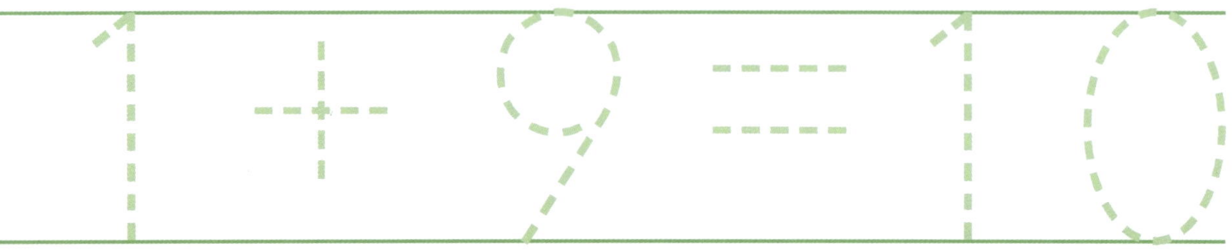

Count the children and complete the sum below.

1 child + 9 children = 10 children

It is Sarah's birthday.
She is turning 10.

Can you draw the missing candles on her cake to make 10?

Practise this number bond.

2 + 8 = 10

Trace this number bond.

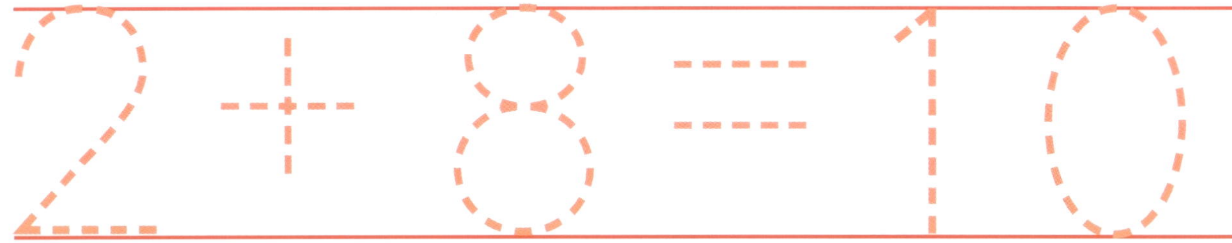

Count the children and complete the sum below.

2 children + 8 children = 10 children

This pizza is missing some pieces of pepperoni.

Can you draw the missing pepperoni to make 10 pieces?

Practise this number bond.

3 + 7 = 10

Trace this number bond.

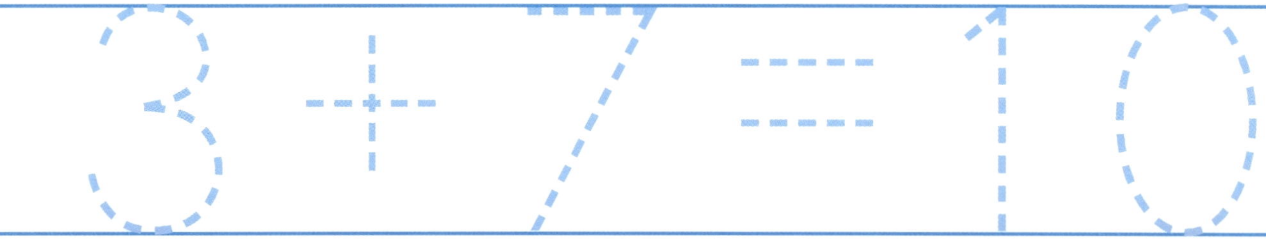

Count the children and complete the sum below.

 children +  children =  children

Alien Al wants 10 spikes on his head, not 3!

Can you draw 7 more spikes?

Practise this number bond.

4 + 6 = 10

Trace this number bond.

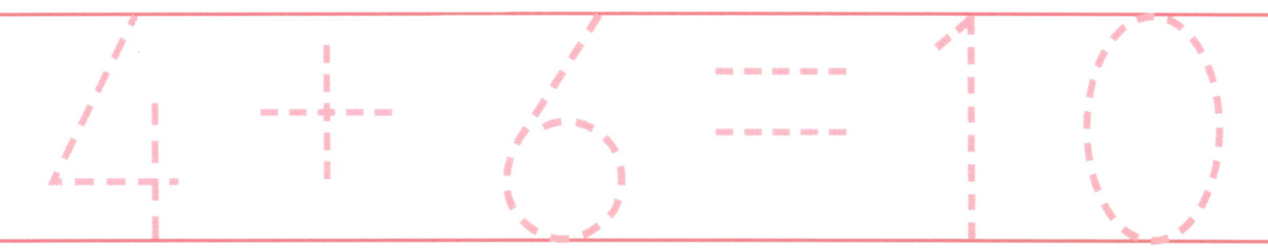

Count the children and complete the sum below.

 children +  children =  children

Danny the dinosaur is missing some teeth.

Can you draw his missing teeth to make 10?

Practise this number bond.

5 + 5 = 10

Trace this number bond.

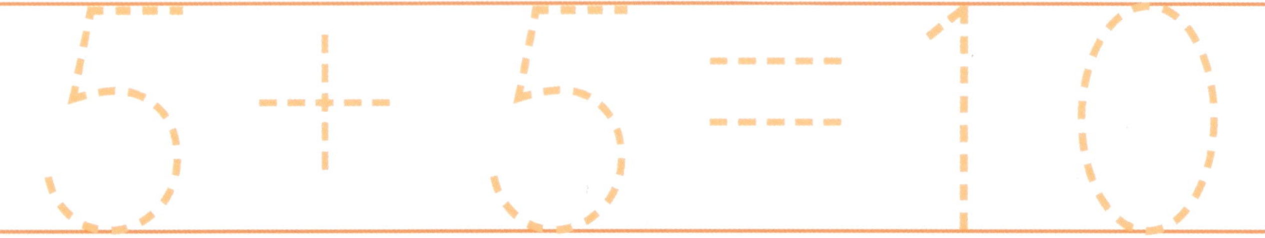

Count the children and complete the sum below.

 children +  children =  children

This ladybird is missing some spots.

Can you draw the missing spots to make 10?

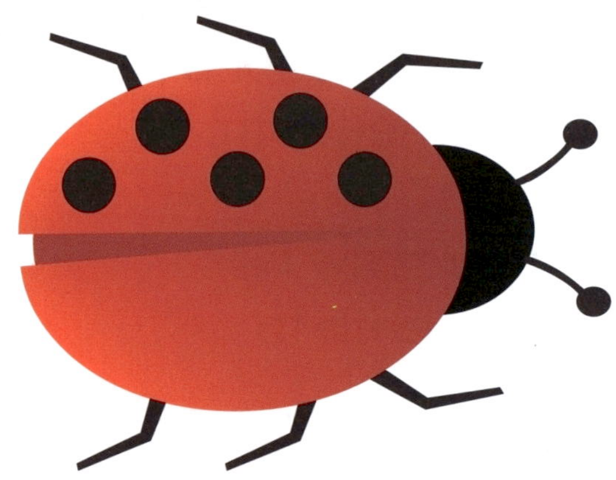

Practise this number bond.

Bonds reversed

Did you know that 0 + 10 = 10 is the same as 10 + 0 = 10?
Each bond can be written in two ways.

10 + 0 = 10   0 + 10 = 10

Trace each bond and its answer.

0 + 10 = 10	10 + 0 = 10
1 + 9 = 10	9 + 1 = 10
2 + 8 = 10	8 + 2 = 10
3 + 7 = 10	7 + 3 = 10
4 + 6 = 10	6 + 4 = 10
5 + 5 = 10	5 + 5 = 10

6 + 4 = 10

Trace this number bond.

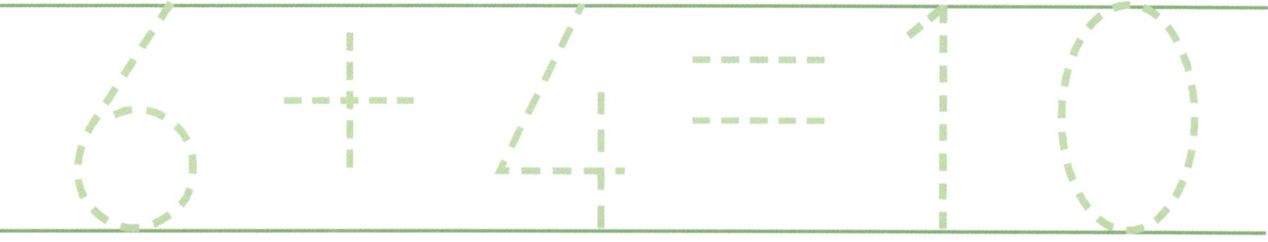

Count the children and complete the sum below.

children +

children =

children

Bill's dinner plate is missing some peas.

Can you draw the missing peas to make 10?

Practise this number bond.

7 + 3 = 10

Trace this number bond.

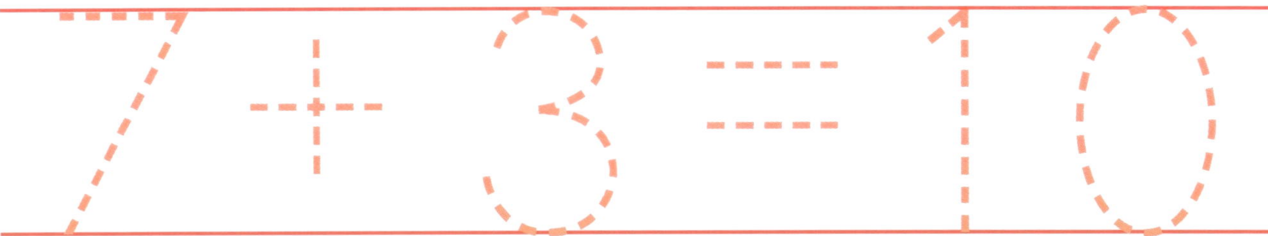

Count the children and complete the sum below.

 children +  children =  children

This garden should have 10 flowers.

Can you draw the missing flowers to make 10?

Practise this number bond.

8 + 2 = 10

Trace this number bond.

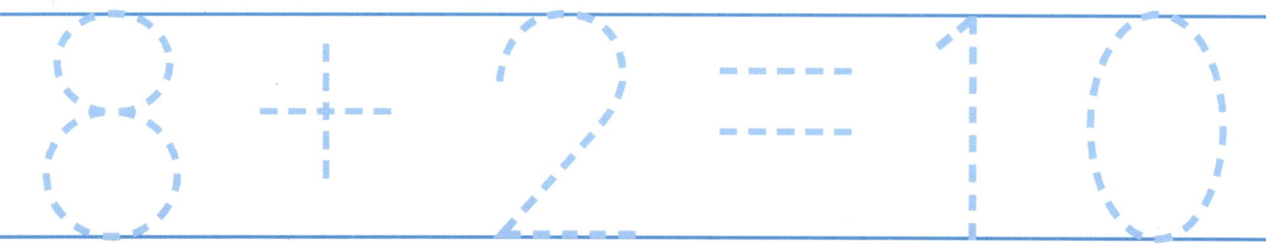

Count the children and complete the sum below.

 children + 2 children =  children

Some cupcakes are missing their cherries.

Can you draw the missing cherries to make 10?

Practise this number bond.

9 + 1 = 10

Trace this number bond.

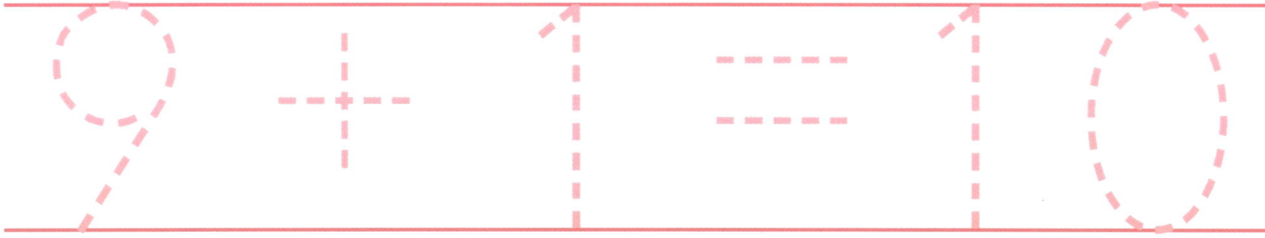

Count the children and complete the sum below.

 children +  child =  children

This frog needs to get across the pond.

Can you draw the 1 missing lily pad to make 10?

Practise this number bond.

10 + 0 = 10

Trace this number bond.

Count the children and complete the sum below.

 children +  children = 10 children

How many jewels are there on the crown?

Trace over the dotted line to complete the picture of the crown.

Practise this number bond.

Octopus maths

Ollie Octopus loves the number 10. Can you write the number bonds to 10 on his long legs?

Addition

Use the number bonds to 10 to solve these problems.
Write the missing numbers in the boxes.

Builder bonds

Draw lines between the two cranes to match up the number bonds to 10. The first one is done for you.

Matching socks

Draw lines between the socks that make a number bond to 10.

Bone hunt

Can you match the dogs and their bones to their kennel homes to make the number bonds to 10?

Subtraction

Number bonds can be used to help you solve problems involving subtraction from 10.

Trace over the subtractions.

10 - 0 = 10	10 - 5 = 5
10 - 1 = 9	10 - 6 = 4
10 - 2 = 8	10 - 7 = 3
10 - 3 = 7	10 - 8 = 2
10 - 4 = 6	10 - 9 = 1

Can you see the pattern?

Write the answer in the box below to practise the subtraction problems above.

10 – 5 = ☐

Clever crabs

Can you solve these subtraction problems by writing in the missing numbers?

Caterpillar puzzles

These caterpillars should have 10 shoes on their feet.
Can you figure out how many they are missing?

Benny has only 6 shoes.
How many is he missing?

$10 - 6 = \square$

Sophie has only 2 shoes.
How many is she missing?

$10 - 2 = \square$

Joe has only 5 shoes.
How many is he missing?

$10 - 5 = \square$

Missing numbers

Write in the missing numbers to
to solve the subtractions.

10 − ☐ = 1

10 − ☐ = 4

10 − ☐ = 7

10 − ☐ = 6

10 − ☐ = 2

Counting colours

Following the example, write the number of different coloured toys on each shelf in the boxes below.

Dot-to-dot

Complete the pictures below by joining up the dots.

4 5 6 7

house

3 8

2 9

1 10

Buzzing around

Colour in the busy, buzzy scene. How many bees are buzzing around the beehive?

Drawing numbers

Follow the instructions to complete the number pictures.

Draw two wheels on the car.

Add five spots to the dice.

Draw six whiskers on the kitten.

Add three more flowers to the bunch.

Spot the difference

Can you spot the five differences between the two builder's bags? Then colour in both tool bags.

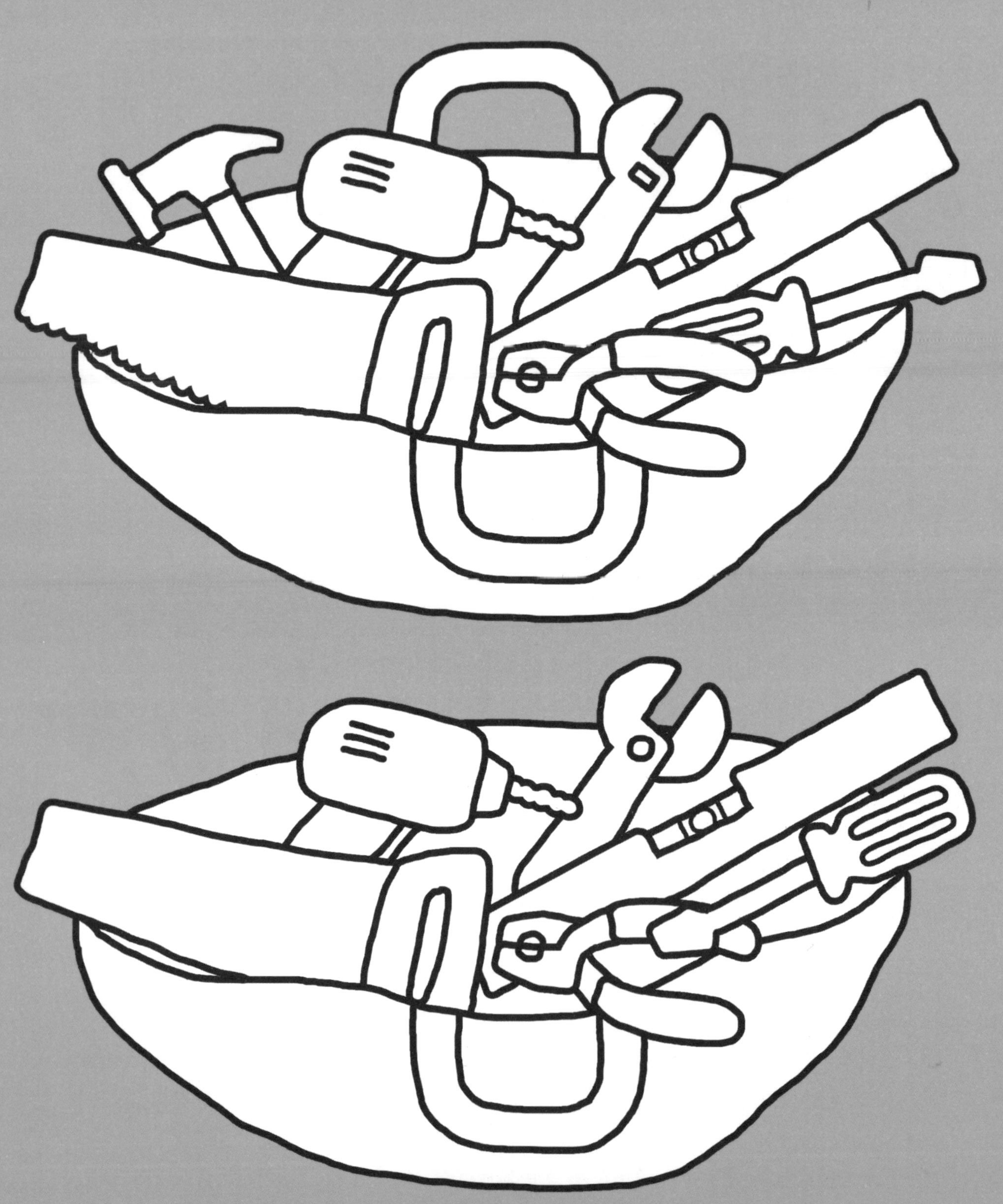

Tracing

Trace along the dotted lines of each of the shapes below.

Palm pirates

How many coconuts are in the tree?
Colour in the pirate scene.

Outer space

This space picture contains lots of different shapes. Can you find them all? Tick the boxes when you find them.

triangle ☐ **circle** ☐

square ☐

star ☐ **rectangle** ☐

Spooky counting

Count and circle the objects below when you find them all.

five shiny keys

four green toads

three blue potions

two hairy spiders

one wizard hat

How to use this book

Children develop skills at different times and this book is designed to support them as they grow and learn. The pen control and writing activities will allow children to practise holding a pen and the sticker activities will encourage fine motor skills.

Holding a pen

Encourage your child to hold a pen in between the thumb and the index finger, a little above the tip, with a gap in between. Left-handers should hold the pen slightly further up from the tip, as shown in the picture.

The pen should be resting on the middle finger to support it. It should be easy for your child to move the pen up and down by moving those three fingers only.

Right hand or left hand

You probably know by now which hand your child favours. If not, this book will help. You will probably notice better pen control with one, although some people are happy to use both.

Fingers should flex, not the arm.

Don't press down too hard.

Perfect posture

It is best for your child to sit at a flat table or desk, feet on the floor with back straight. For right-handers, the book should be at a slight angle, on the right side of your child's body. For left-handers, the book should be positioned at more of an angle on the left side of the body, with the top left corner about two inches higher than the right.

ant

apple

look at the letter

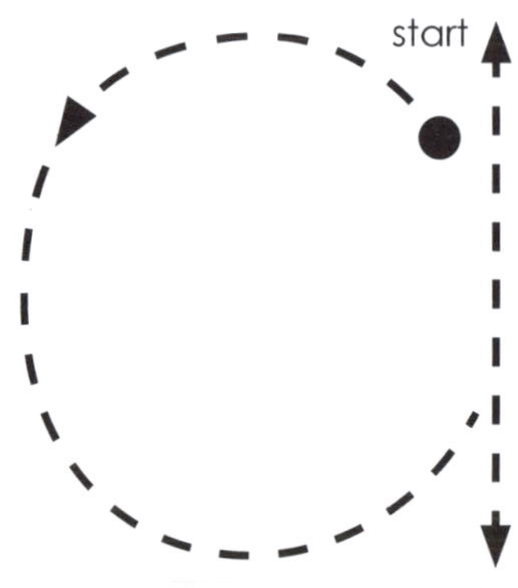

trace the letter

write inside

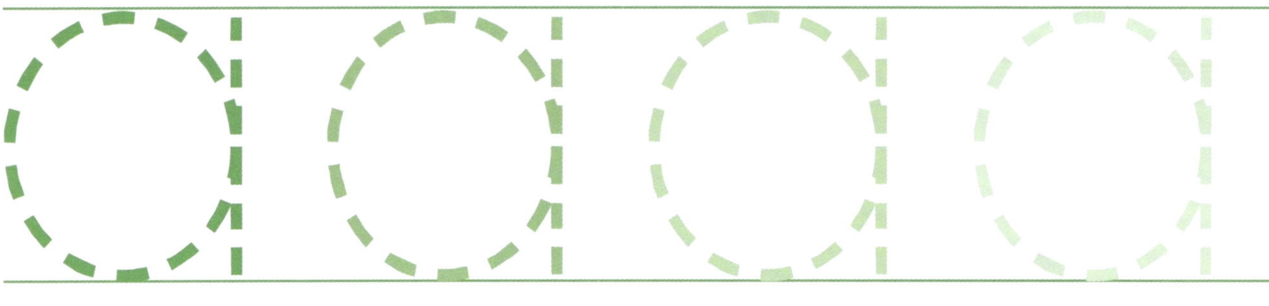

letter practice

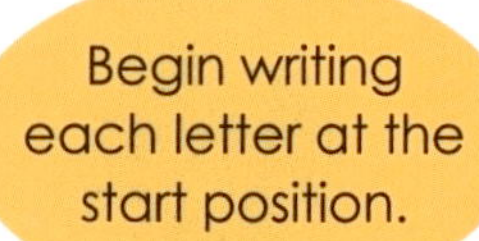

butterfly

ball

look at the letter

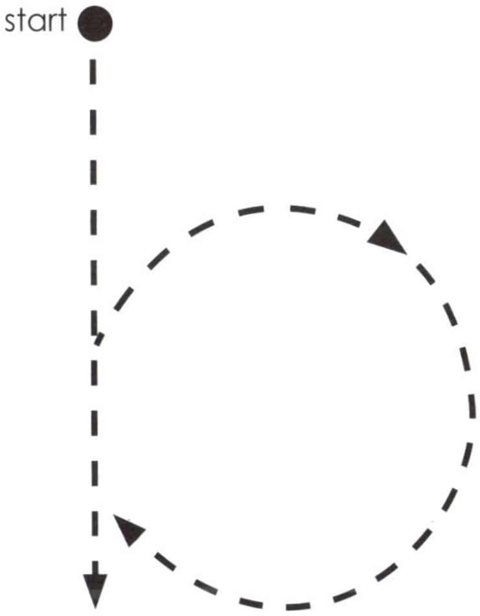

trace the letter

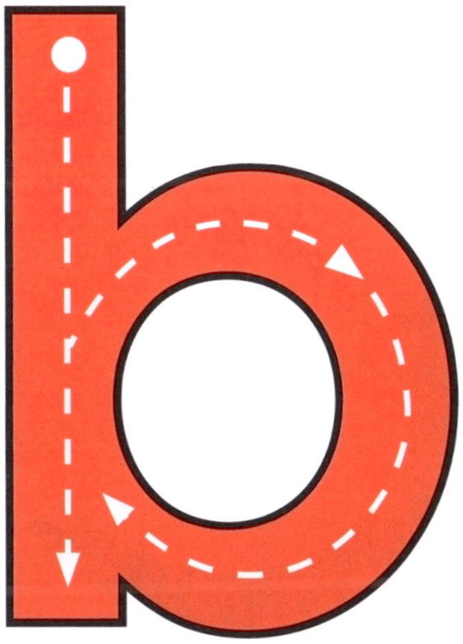

start

write inside

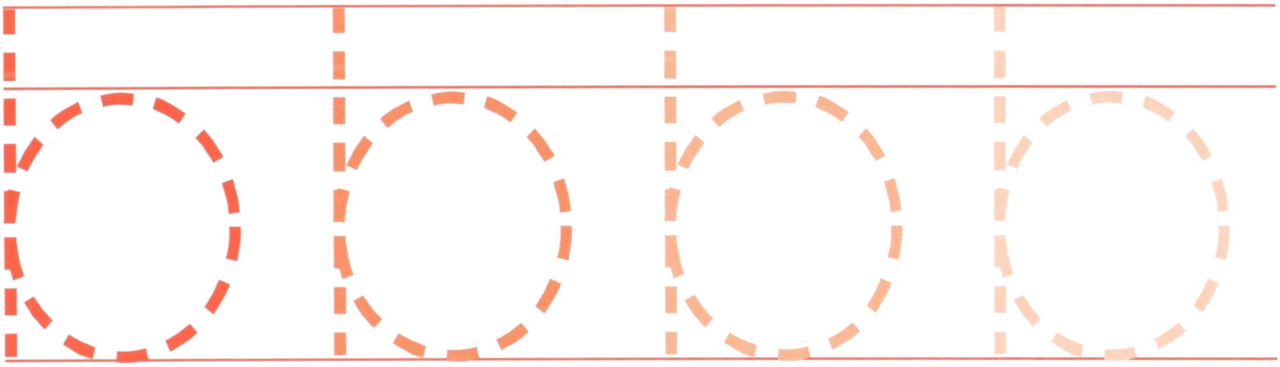

letter practice

cat

cupcake

look at the letter

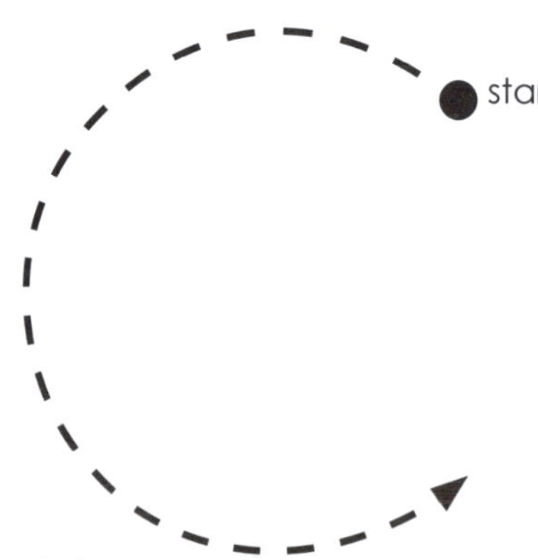

trace the letter

write inside

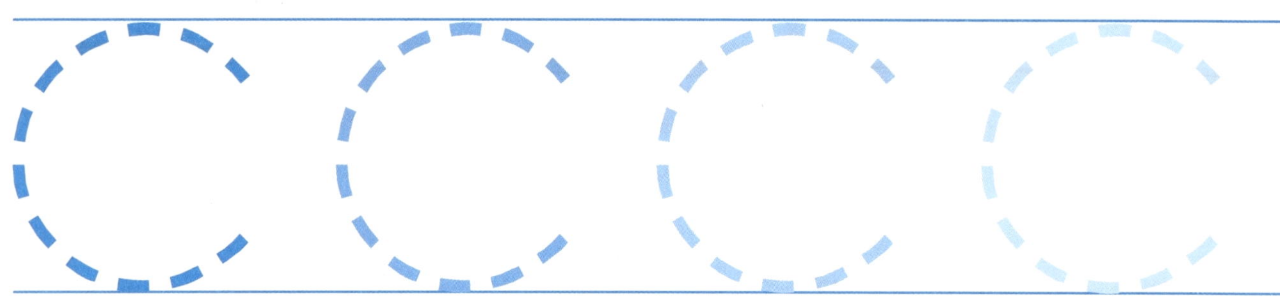

Take it slow and steady.

letter practice

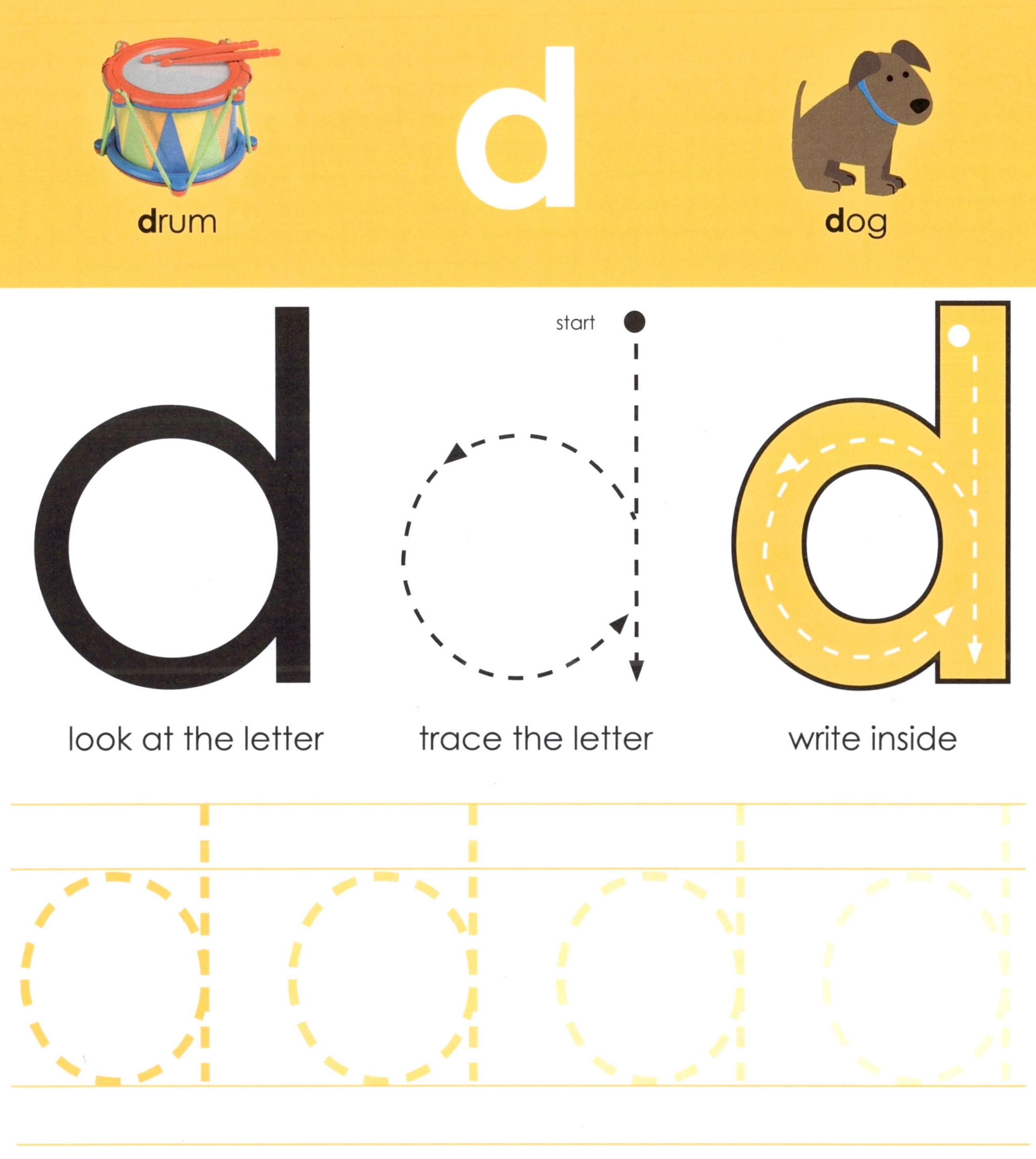

letter practice

egg

elephant

look at the letter

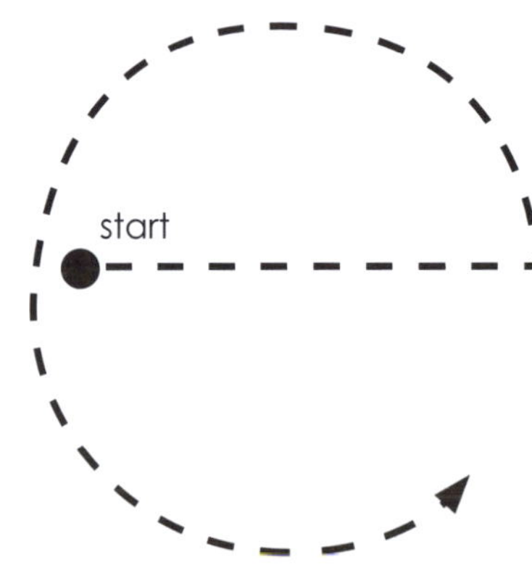

trace the letter

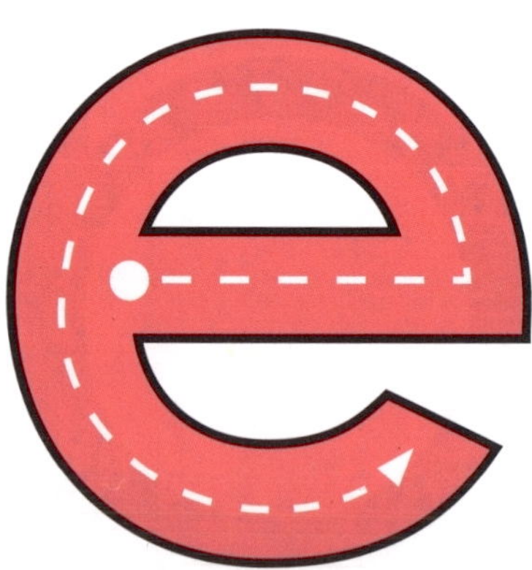

write inside

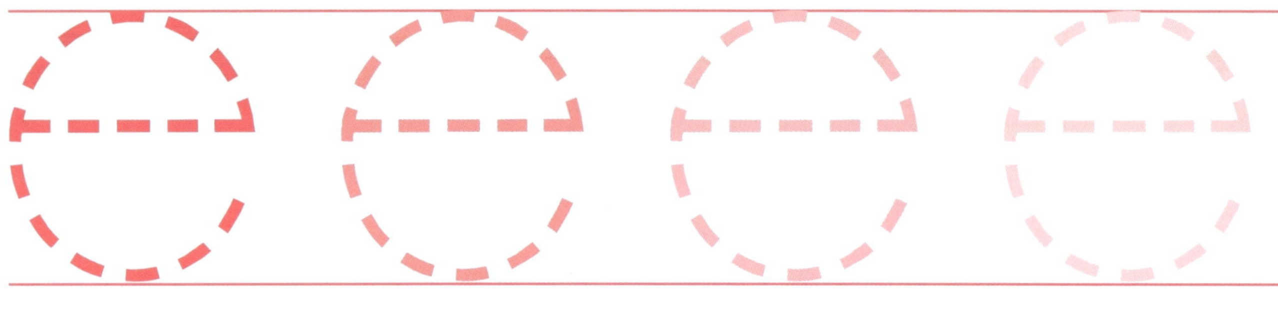

letter practice

letter practice

goat

grapes

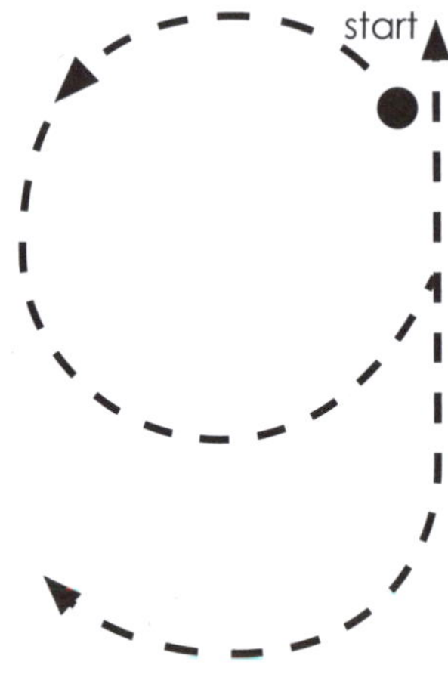

look at the letter

trace the letter

write inside

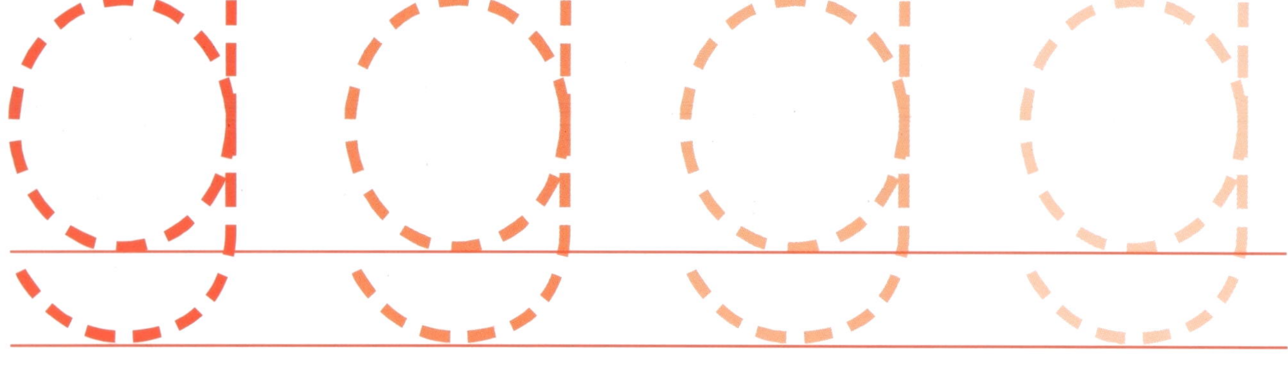

letter practice

hat

horse

look at the letter

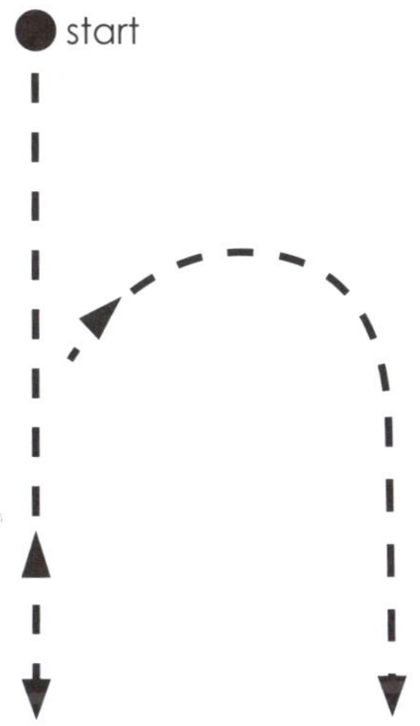

trace the letter

write inside

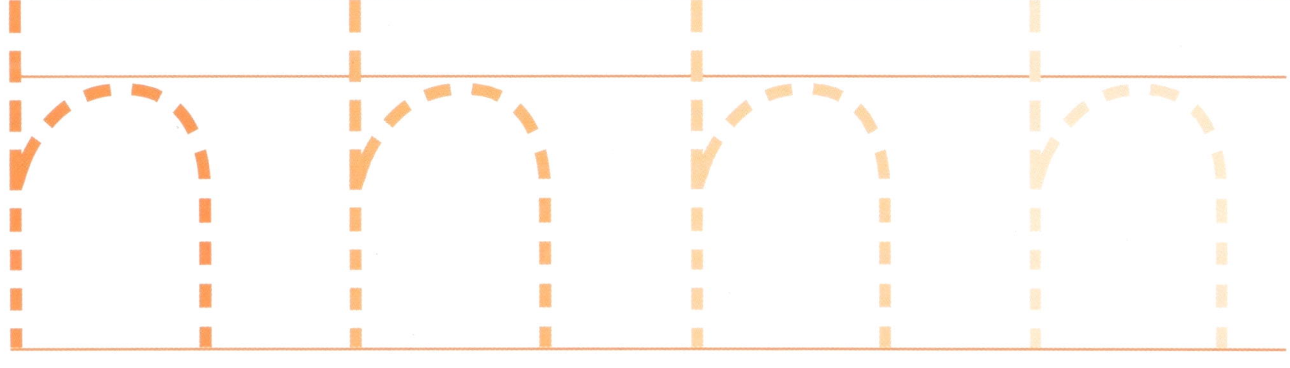

Start at the top line.

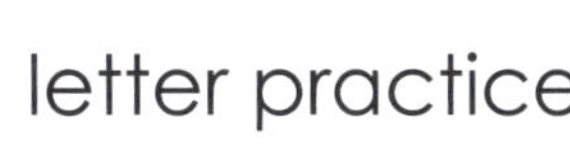

letter practice

letter practice

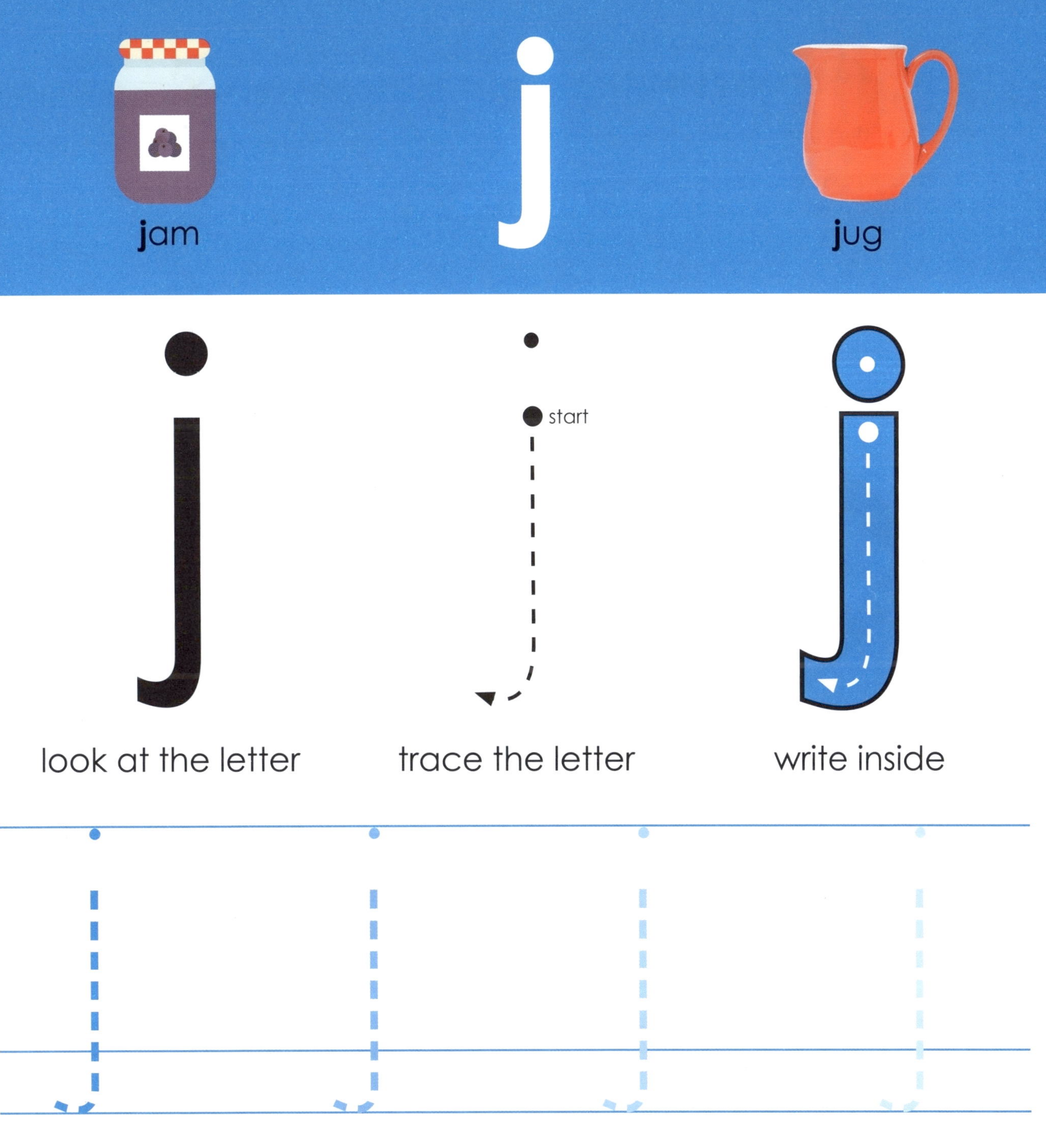

letter practice

look at the letter

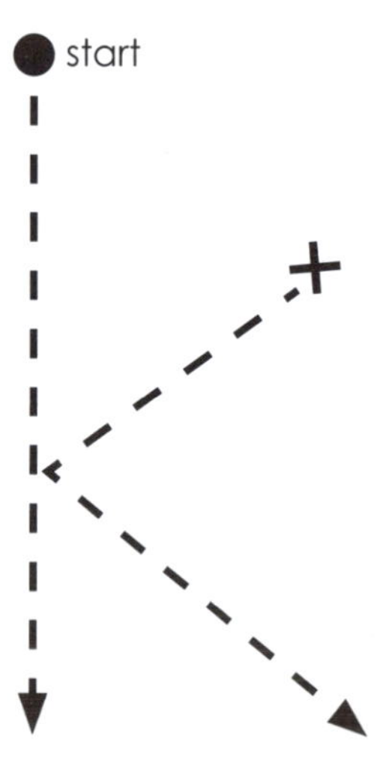

trace the letter

write inside

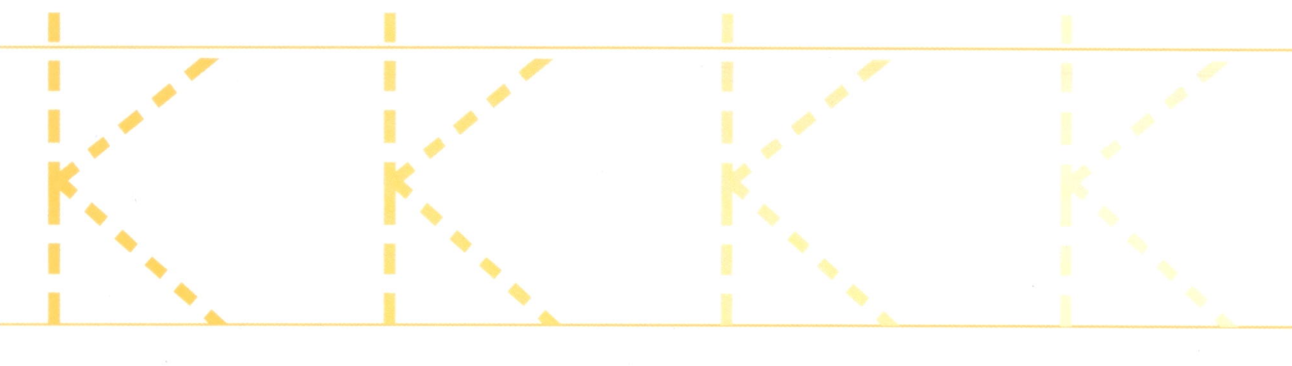

Great writing!

letter practice

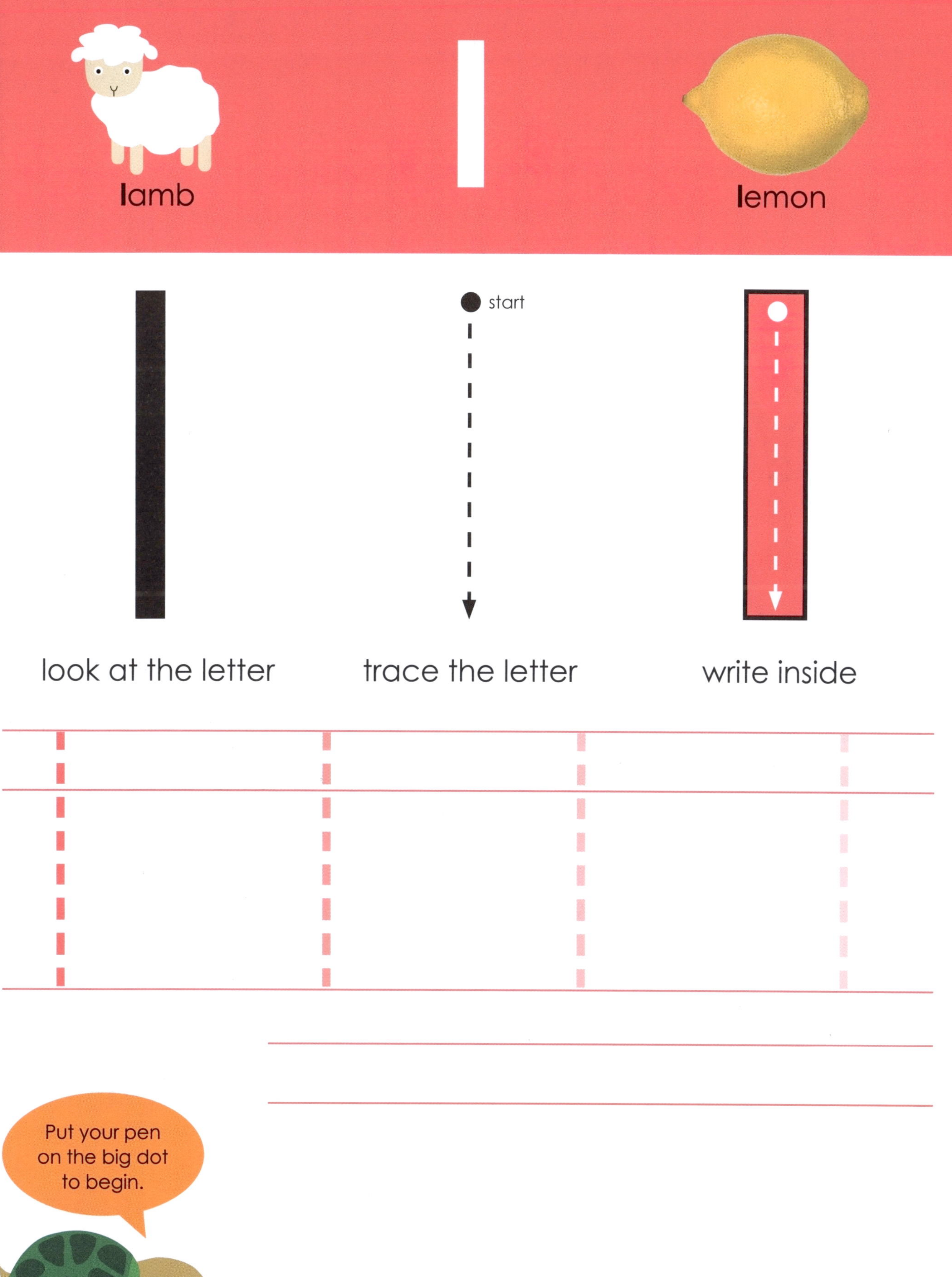
lamb
l
lemon
start
look at the letter
trace the letter
write inside
letter practice
Put your pen
on the big dot
to begin.

milk

moon

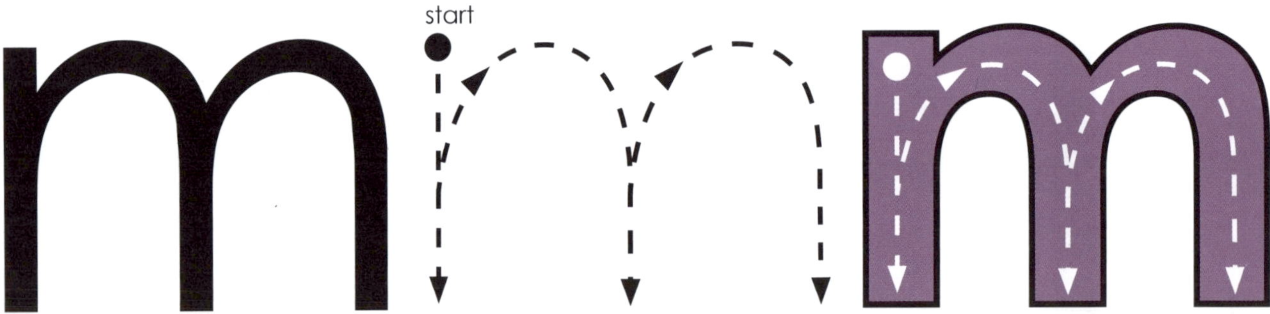

look at the letter

trace the letter

write inside

letter practice

nest

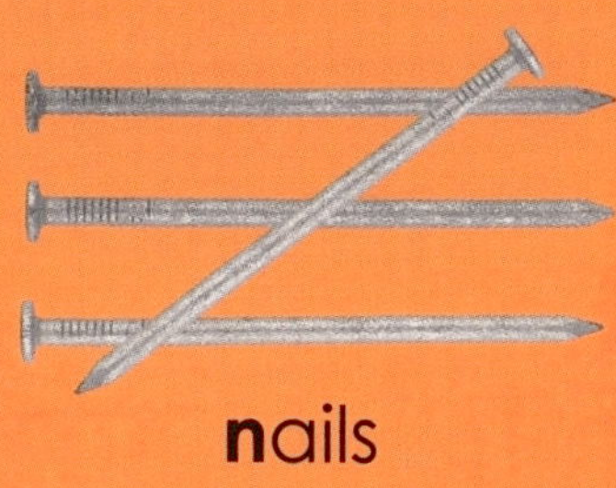

nails

look at the letter

trace the letter

write inside

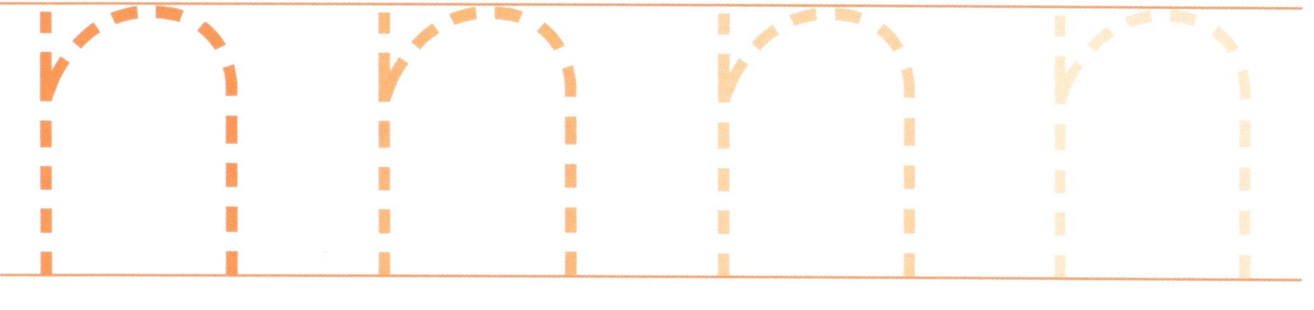

letter practice

orange

otter

look at the letter

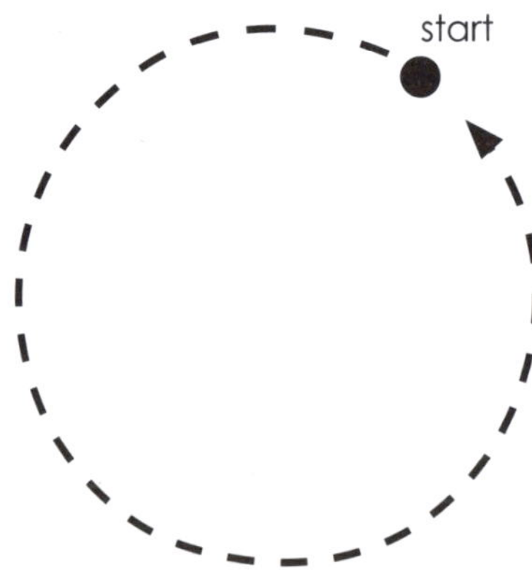

trace the letter

write inside

letter practice

piglet

pear

start

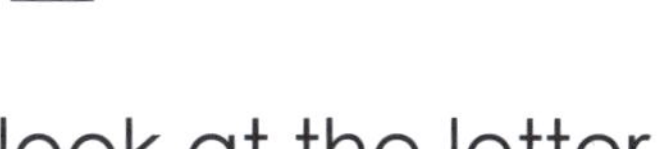

look at the letter

trace the letter

write inside

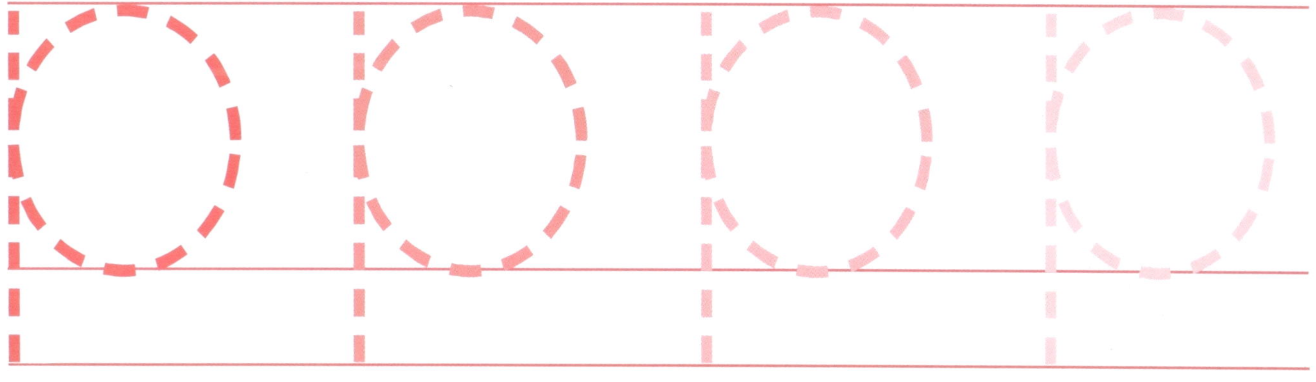

The long stick on the **p** goes below the line.

letter practice

queen

quiet

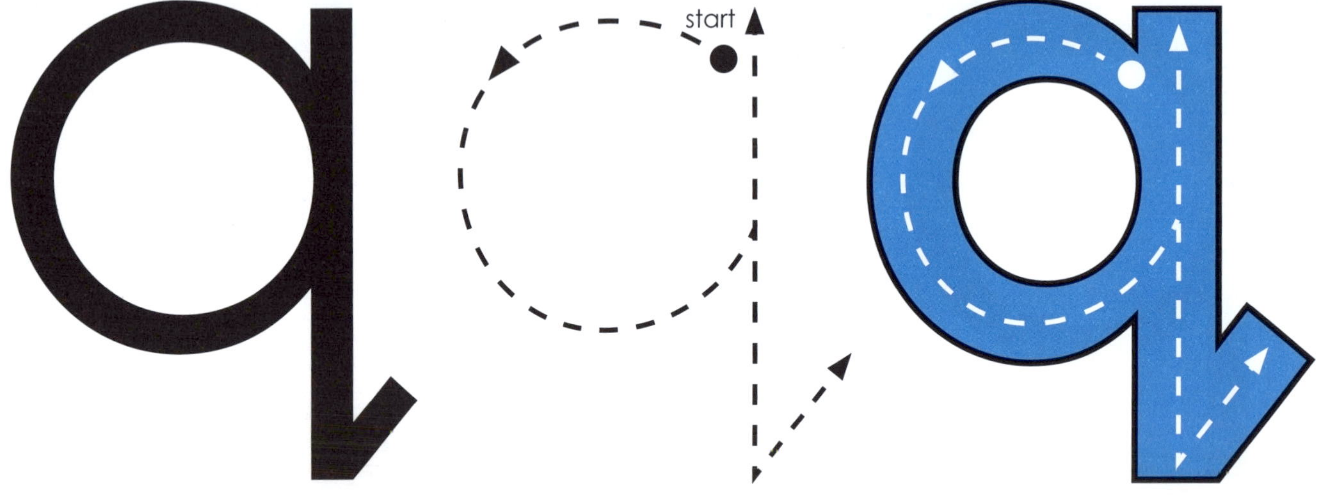

look at the letter

trace the letter

write inside

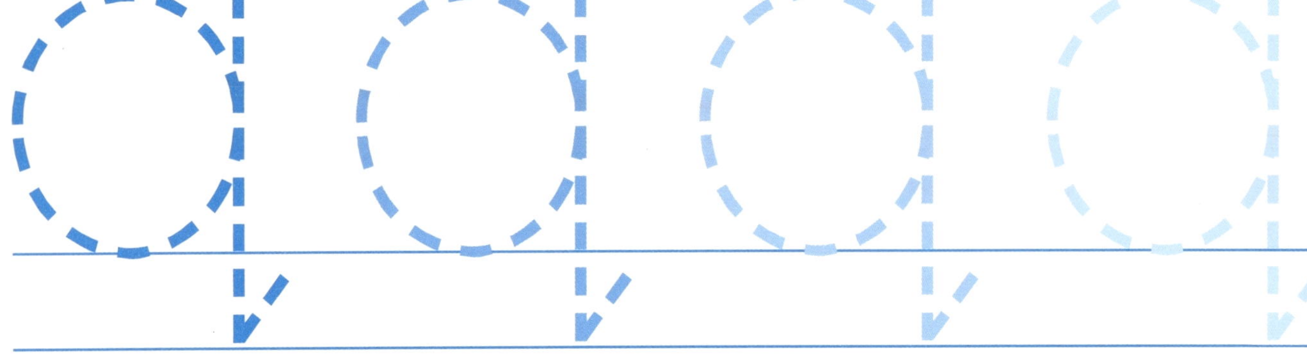

letter practice

rose

rabbit

look at the letter

trace the letter

write inside

letter practice

snake

s

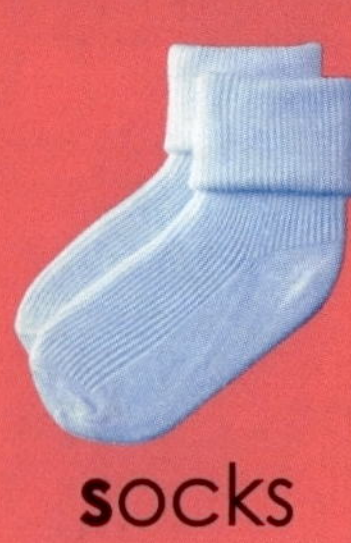

socks

look at the letter

trace the letter

write inside

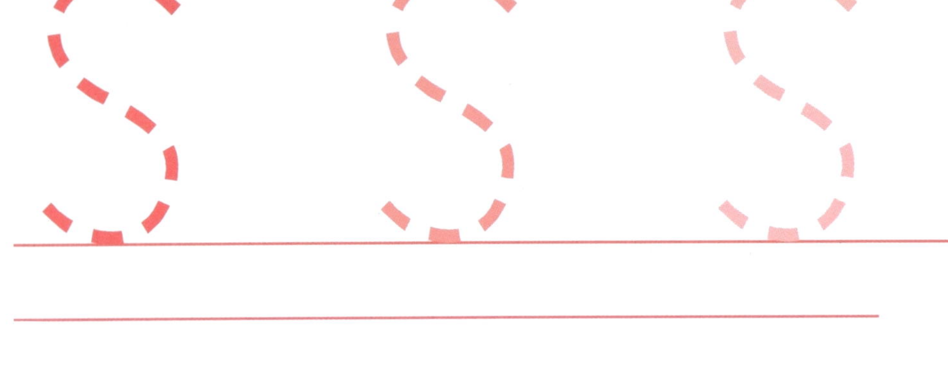

letter practice

letter practice

up

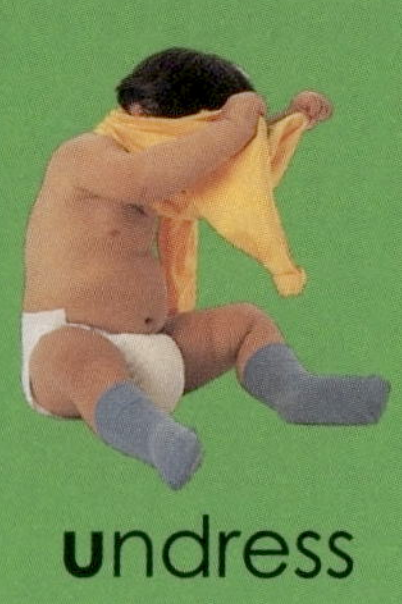

undress

look at the letter

start

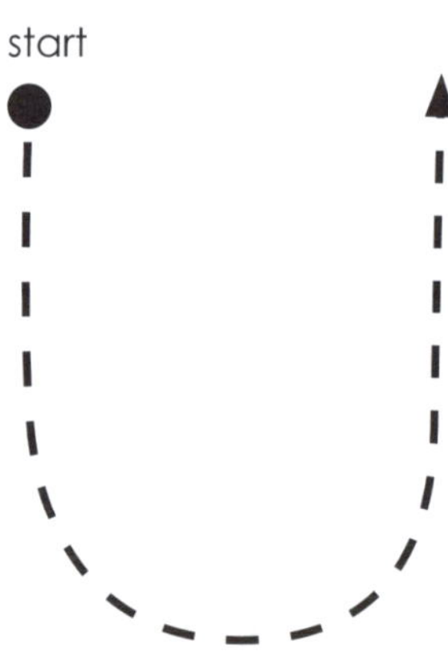

trace the letter

write inside

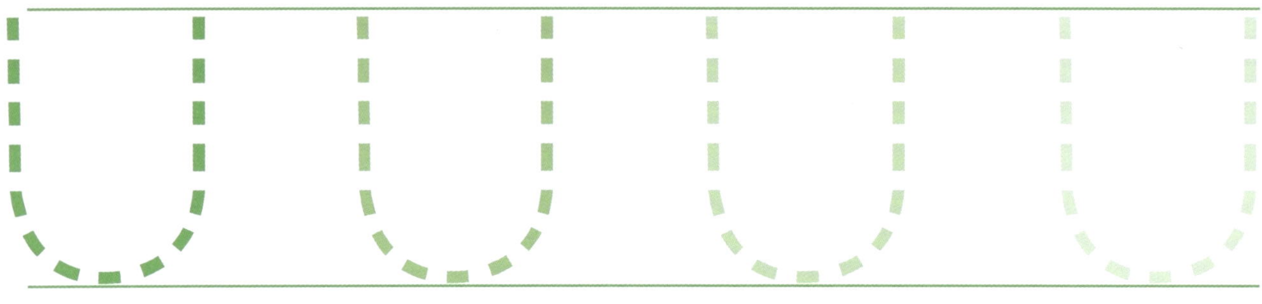

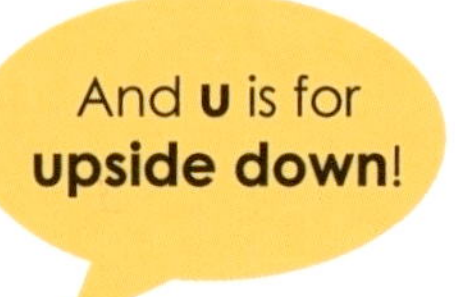

letter practice

vase

violin

start

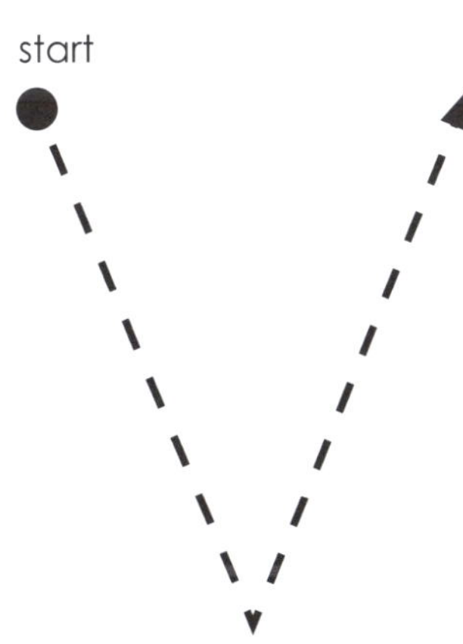

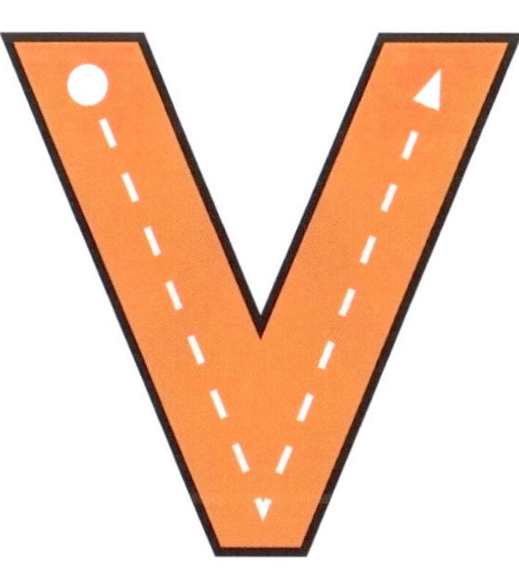

look at the letter

trace the letter

write inside

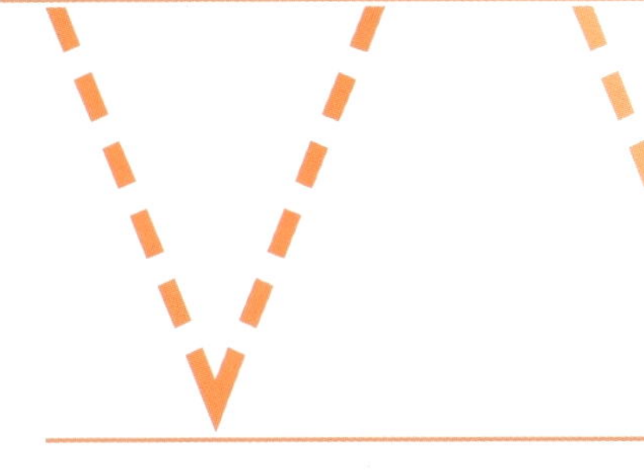

letter practice

watermelon

whale

look at the letter

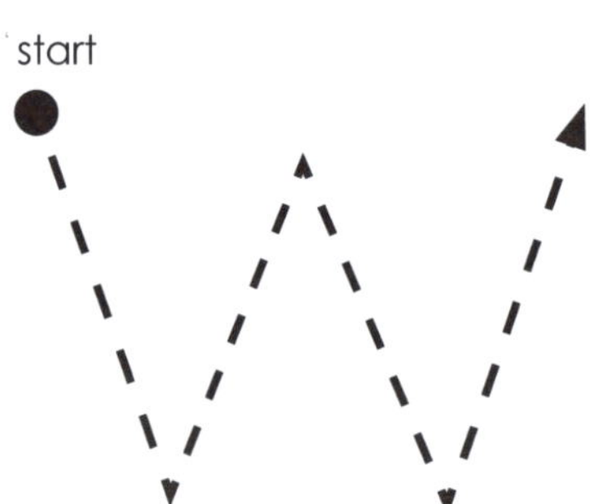

trace the letter

write inside

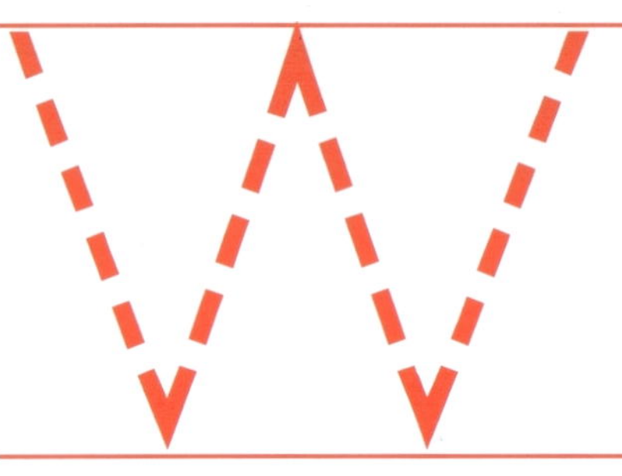

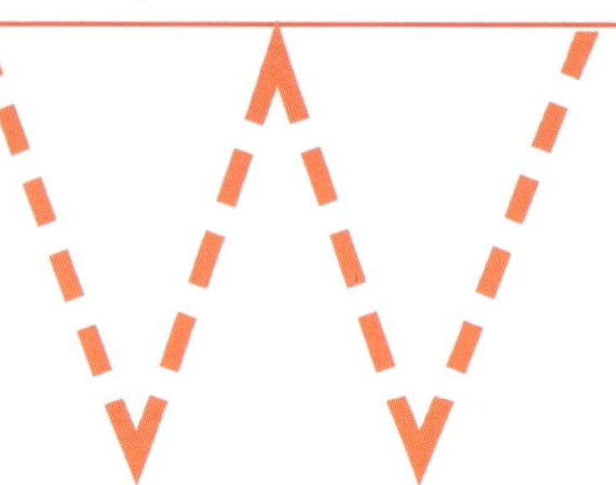

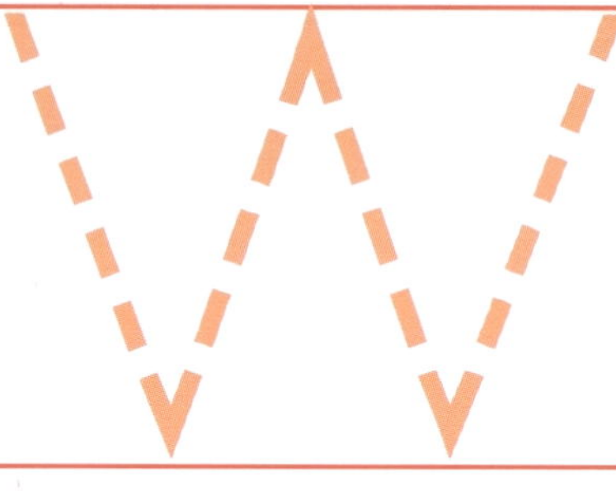

letter practice

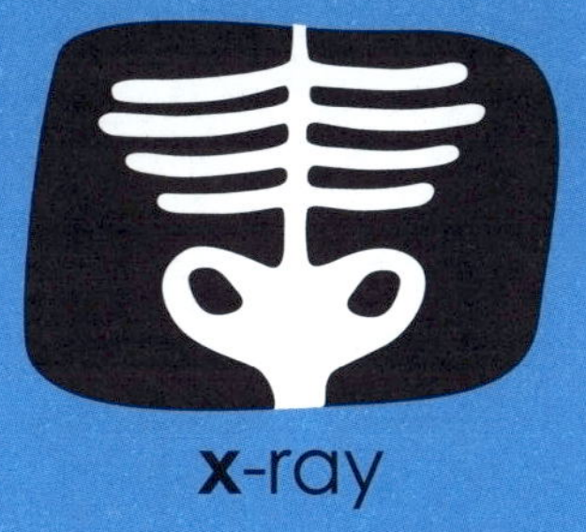

x-ray

xylophone

look at the letter

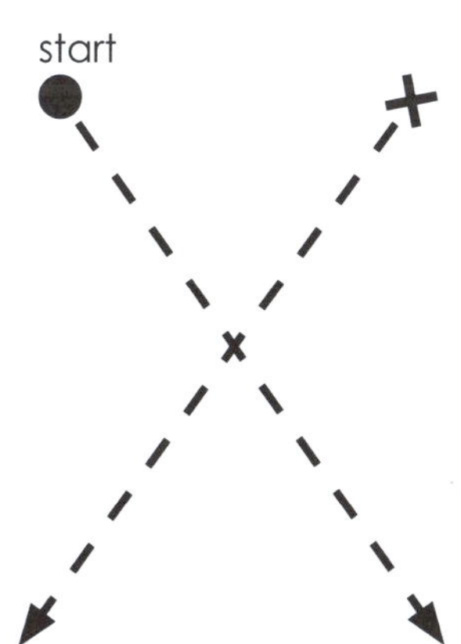

trace the letter

write inside

letter practice

yo-yo

yawn

y

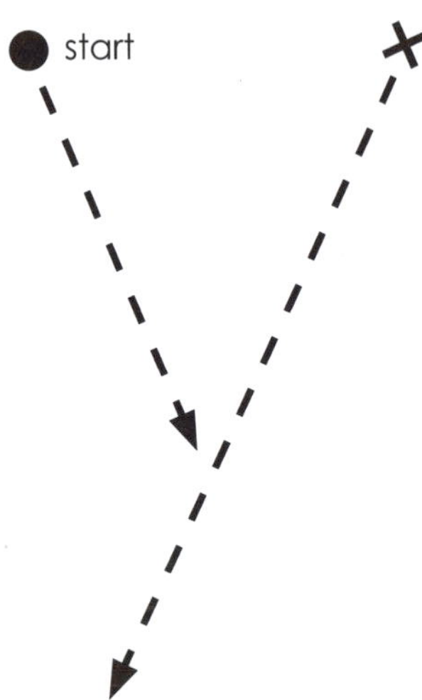

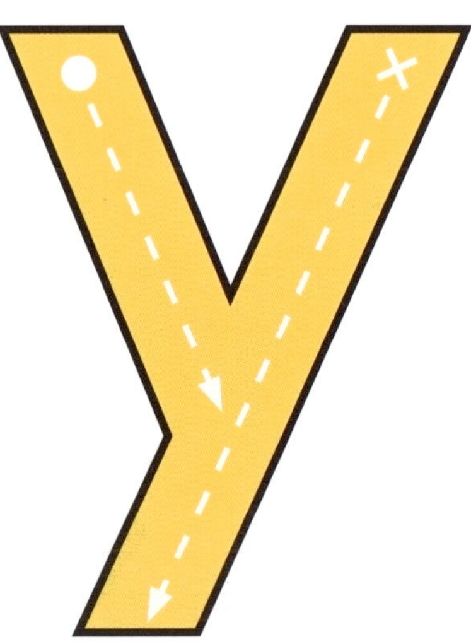

look at the letter

trace the letter

write inside

Take the pen down to the bottom line.

letter practice

zoo

z

zigzag

Z

look at the letter

start

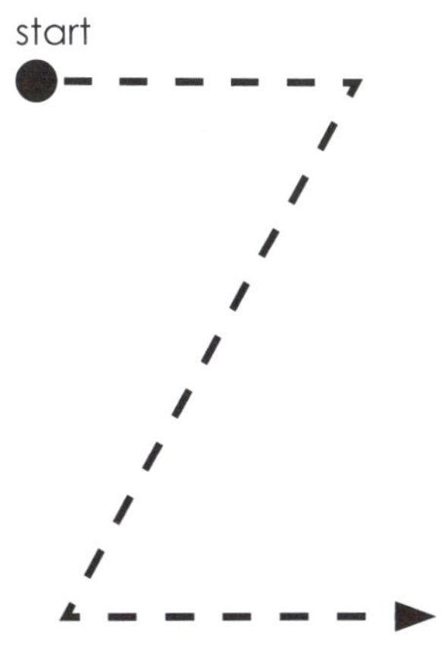

trace the letter

write inside

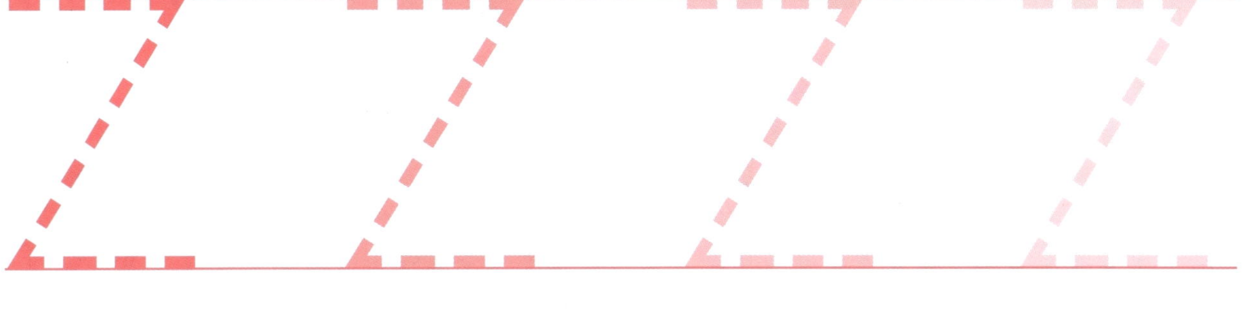

letter practice

Dino jungle

This dino picture needs some colour.
Which dinosaur is the scariest?

At the farm

Write over the names of the things we get from the farm.

Pretty butterfly

Colour in the butterfly to match its friend.

Farm maze

Follow the green lines to find the quickest way through the maze to get the tractor to the barn.

In the toy box

Colour in the toys below.
Can you circle all the dolls?

I spy...

Match each animal to the letter it begins with.

Tracing lines

Trace the dotted lines from top to bottom.

start

Can you complete the balloon strings?

start

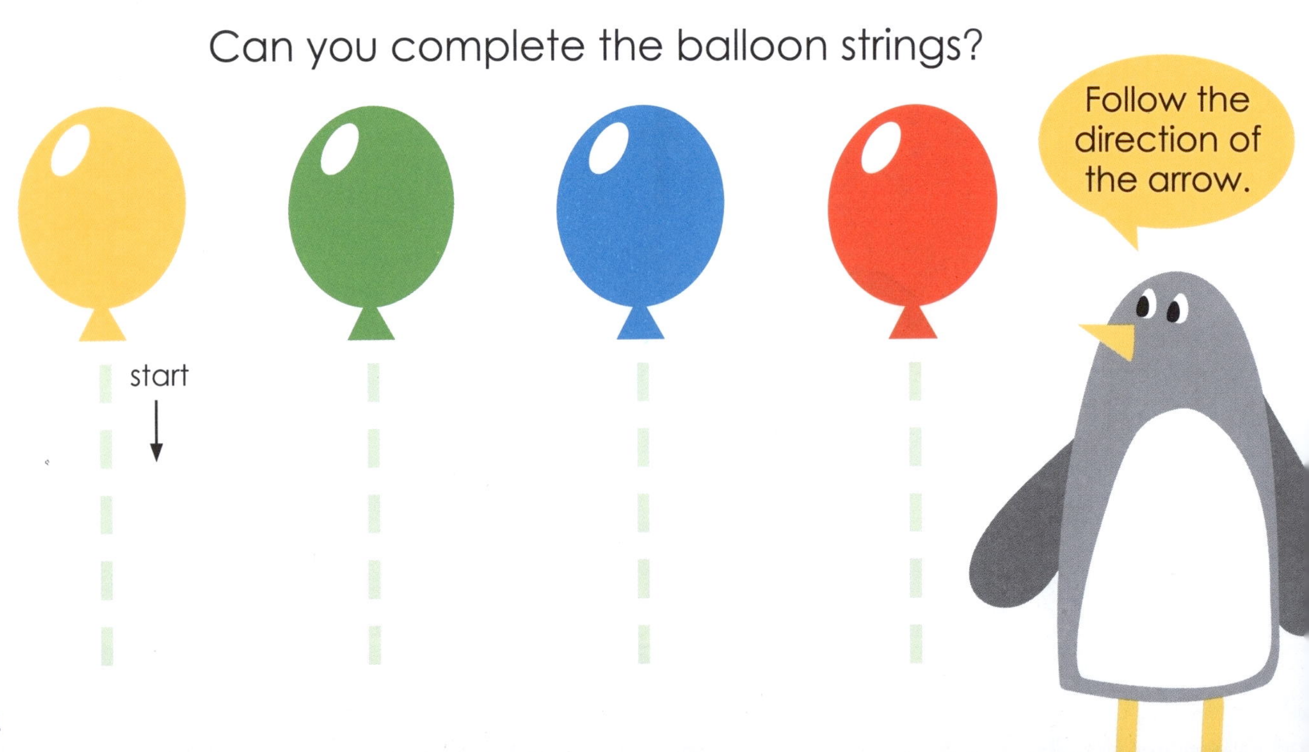

Curves

Trace the dotted lines down and around.

start

Can you complete the skipping ropes?

Diagonals

Trace the dotted lines from top to bottom.

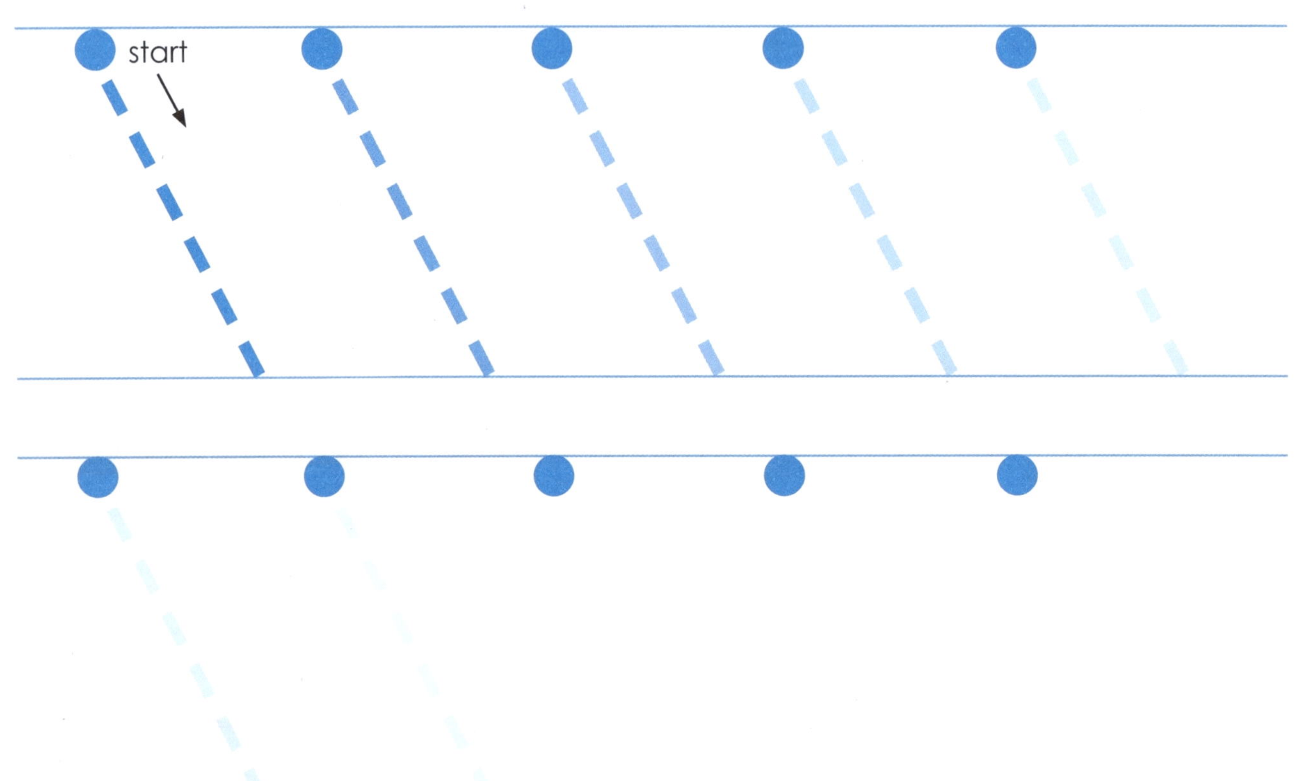

Can you complete the kite strings?

Across

Trace the dotted lines from left to right.

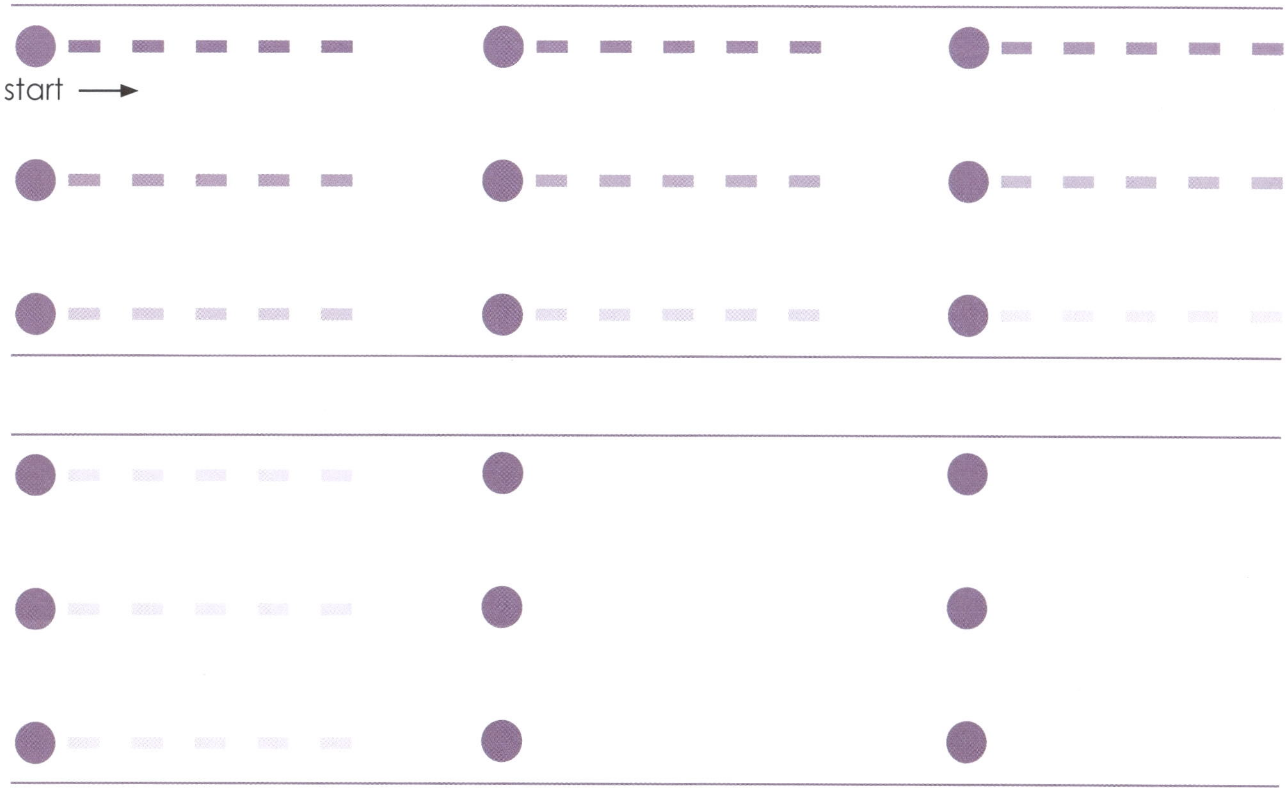

start →

Can you complete the arrows?

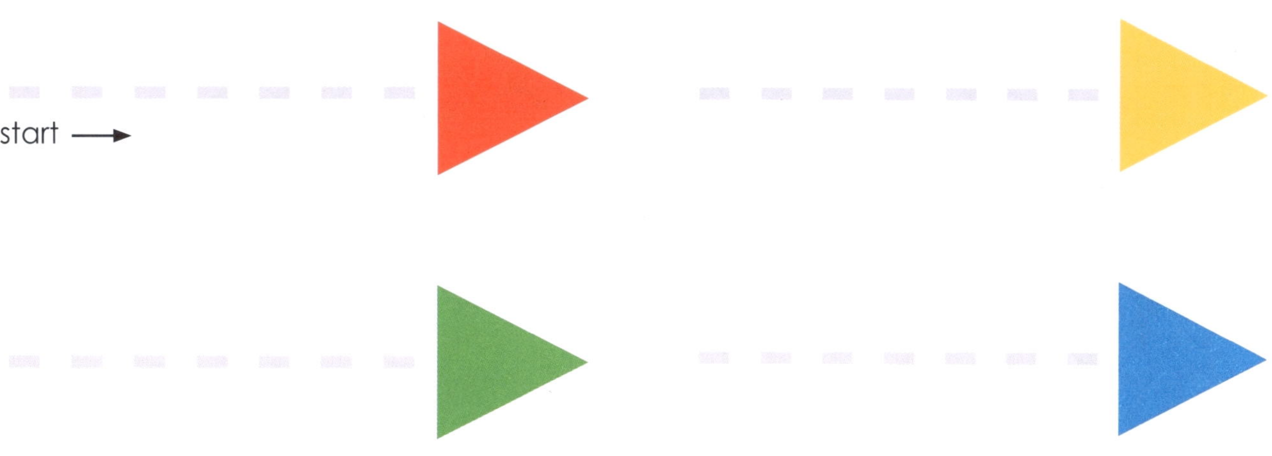

Curved line patterns

Trace along the lines from the animals to their favourite snacks.

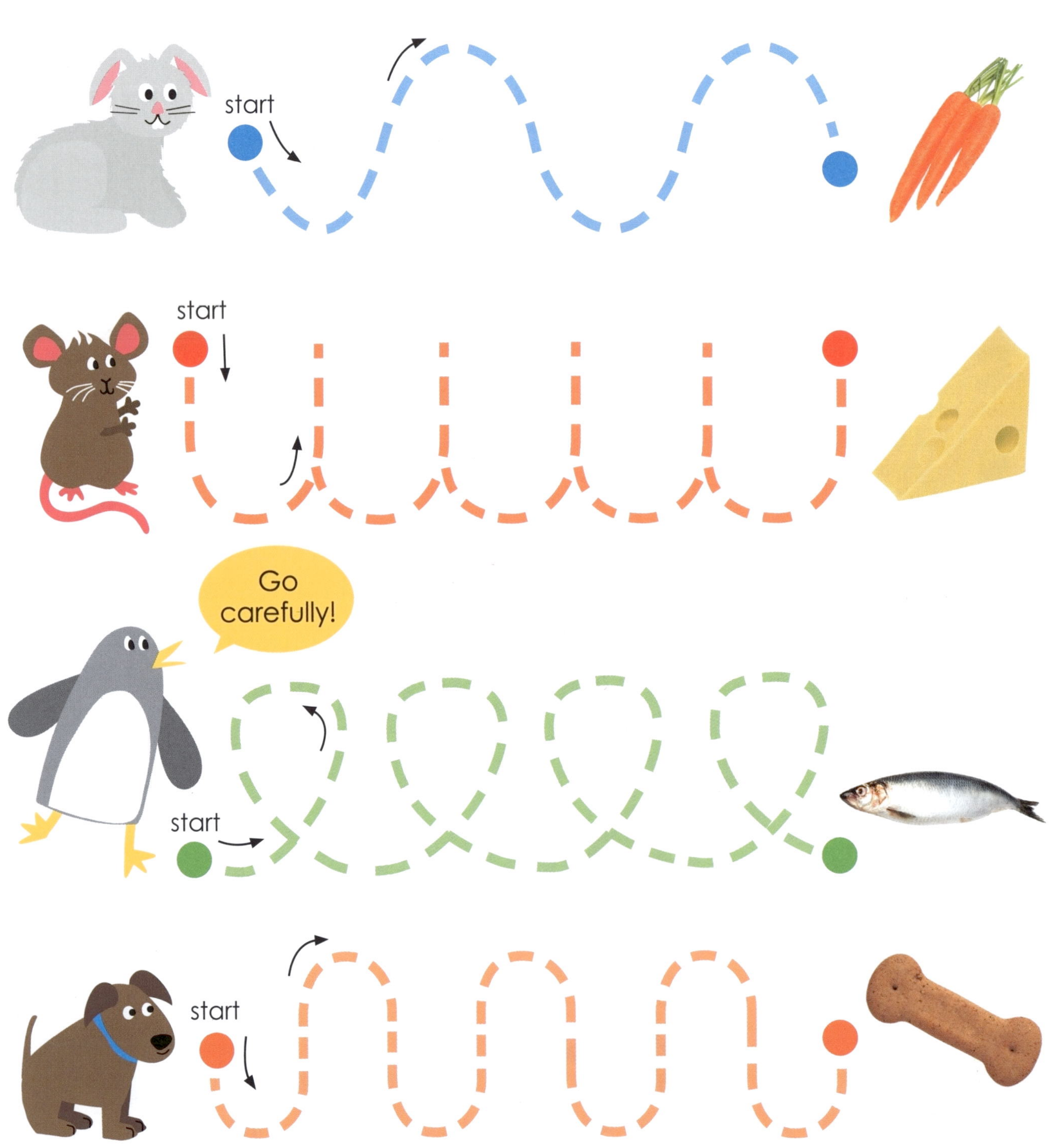

Straight line patterns

Trace along the lines from the children to their belongings.

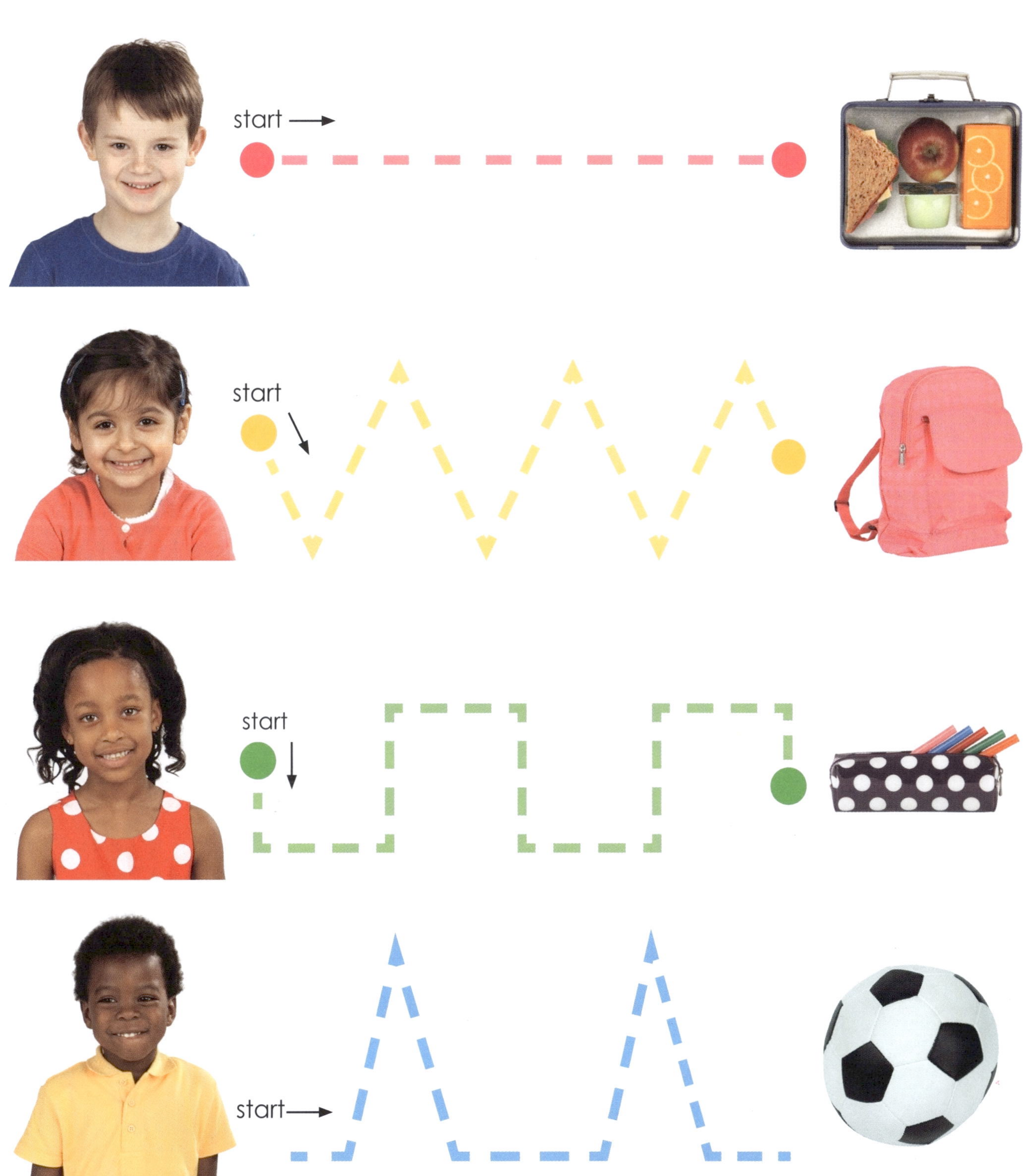

Race day

Help these race cars to the finishing flags.

Animal sorting

Put a cross on all the animals that don't have four legs.
The first one has been done as an example.

Linking lines

Draw a line through all the red and green apples from start to finish.

Squares

Look at the square.

Trace the square.

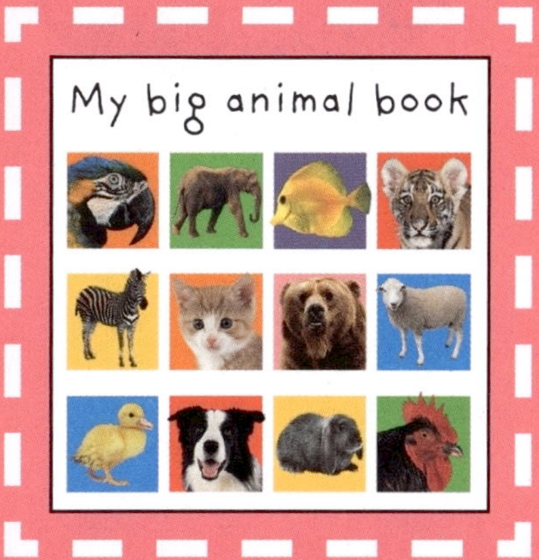

Can you trace around these square-shaped things?

Circles

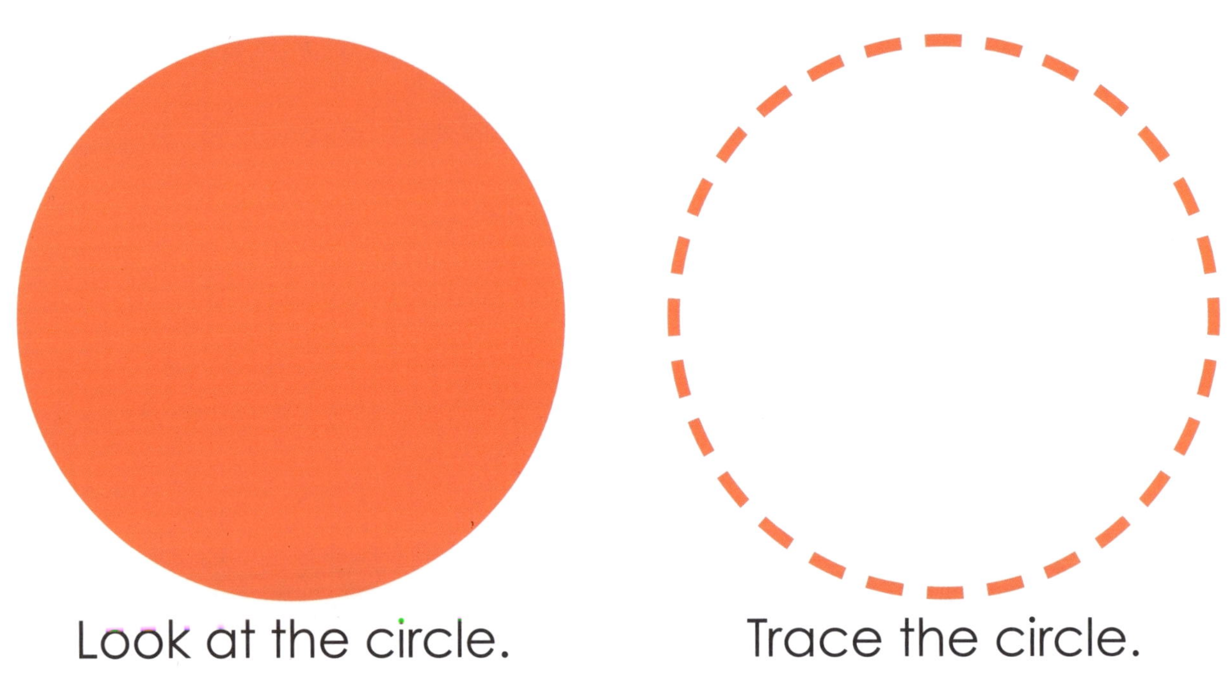

Look at the circle.

Trace the circle.

Can you trace around these circle-shaped things?

Triangles

Look at the triangle. Trace the triangle.

Can you trace around these triangle-shaped things?

Rectangles

Look at the rectangle.

Trace the rectangle.

Can you trace around these rectangle-shaped things?

Hearts

Look at the heart.

Trace the heart.

Can you trace around these heart-shaped things?

Stars

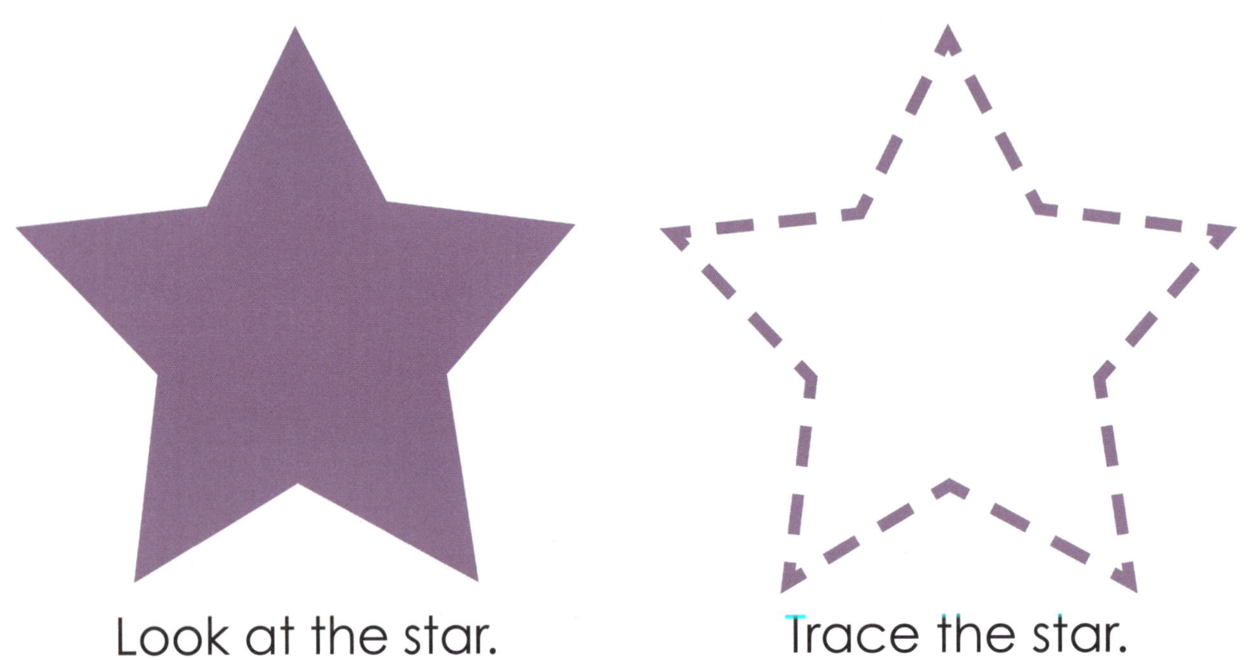

Look at the star.

Trace the star.

Can you trace around these star-shaped things?

Safari trail

Draw a line along the correct footprint path
to get to the lion.

On the tracks

Trace over the lines to draw a train.
Can you add the steam yourself?

Dinosaur path

Help the Carnotaurus find the Triceratops by drawing a line inside the path from start to finish.

Ski slope

Trace along the zigzag tracks made by each skiing penguin.

Animal patterns

Draw lines to match each close-up to the correct animal.

tiger

zebra

goldfish

giraffe

Loop the loop

Help the plane practise its loop the loops by tracing along the line.

Follow me

Draw a line over all the yellow ducks from start to finish.

Outer space

Trace over the shapes to complete the space scene.

Candy craze

Draw a line through the sweet maze
from start to finish.

Alien symmetry

Complete each alien by drawing the other side.

Make a pizza

Add the shaped toppings to the pizza to make it really tasty.

pineapple onions pepperoni pepper

The little mermaid

Colour in this scene of the little mermaid
and her underwater friends.

First sounds

Draw a circle around the things that begin with the letter in each box.

Blast-off!

Add some more stars and planets to this space scene, then colour it in!

Hidden picture

Look at this shop scene.
Can you find the objects pictured below?
Tick the boxes when you find them.

Spot the difference

There are five differences between the two prehistoric pictures.
Circle them when you spot them.